## ALSO BY TAVIS SMILEY

### Books

**What I Know For Sure:** My Story of Growing Up in America

**Covenant with Black America**—Edited by Tavis Smiley

**THE COVENANT In Action**—Compiled by Tavis Smiley

**ACCOUNTABLE:** Making America as Good as Its Promise
—Edited by Tavis Smiley and Stephanie Robinson

**Doing What's Right:** How to Fight for What You Believe—
and Make a Difference

**Keeping the Faith**

**Hard Left**

**How to Make Black America Better**—Edited by Tavis Smiley

### DVDs/CDs

**STAND:** a film by Tavis Smiley

**On Air:** The Best of Tavis Smiley
on the Tom Joyner Morning Show 2004–2008
4-CD commemorative set with booklet

■ ■ ■

Please visit the distributor of SmileyBooks:

Hay House USA: www.hayhouse.com®
Hay House Australia: www.hayhouse.com.au
Hay House UK: www.hayhouse.co.uk
Hay House South Africa: www.hayhouse.co.za
Hay House India: www.hayhouse.co.in

# FAIL UP

## 20 Lessons on Building Success from Failure

# TAVIS SMILEY

HIGHLAND PARK PUBLIC LIBRARY
494 LAUREL AVE.
HIGHLAND PARK, IL 60035-2690
847-432-0216

**SMILEYBOOKS**

DISTRIBUTED BY HAY HOUSE, INC.

Carlsbad, California • New York City
London • Sydney • Johannesburg
Vancouver • Hong Kong • New Delhi

153.9
Sm 64

Copyright © 2011 by Tavis Smiley

**Published in the United States by:** SmileyBooks, 250 Park Avenue South, Suite #201, New York, NY 10003 • www.SmileyBooks.com

**Distributed in the United States by:** Hay House, Inc.: www.hayhouse .com • **Published and distributed in Australia by:** Hay House Australia Pty. Ltd.: www.hayhouse.com.au • **Published and distributed in the United Kingdom by:** Hay House UK, Ltd.: www.hayhouse.co.uk • **Published and distributed in the Republic of South Africa by:** Hay House SA (Pty), Ltd.: www.hayhouse.co.za • **Distributed in Canada by:** Raincoast: www.raincoast.com • **Published and distributed in India by:** Hay House Publishers India: www.hayhouse.co.in

*Cover and interior design:* Charles McStravick • *Interior photos: Credits in text*

All rights reserved. No part of this book may be reproduced by any mechanical, photographic, or electronic process, or in the form of a phonographic recording; nor may it be stored in a retrieval system, transmitted, or otherwise be copied for public or private use—other than for "fair use" as brief quotations embodied in articles and reviews—without prior written permission of the publisher.

The opinions set forth herein are those of the author and do not necessarily express the views of the publisher or Hay House, Inc., or any of its affiliates.

Library of Congress Control Number: 2011920259

Hardcover ISBN: 978-1-4019-3390-6
Digital ISBN: 978-1-4019-3392-0

14 13 12 11   4 3 2 1
1st edition, May 2011

Printed in the United States of America

FSC
www.fsc.org
MIX
Packaging from
responsible sources
FSC® C008955

# CONTENTS

# AUTHOR'S NOTE

This is a work of nonfiction.
Conversations have been
reconstructed to the best
of my recollection.

# INTRODUCTION

*"If I can help somebody as I pass along,*
*If I can cheer somebody with a word or song,*
*If I can show somebody he is traveling wrong,*
*then my living shall not be in vain."*

—DR. MARTIN LUTHER KING, JR.

This book is being released on the occasion of my 20th anniversary in broadcasting: two decades of strife, struggle, and success made more relevant through my many failures.

Most people who have ever succeeded in any human endeavor will tell you they learned more from their failures than they ever learned from their successes. If they're being honest. But a funny thing happens when success becomes an individual's dominant definer. It's what Dr. King, whom I consider the greatest American this country has ever produced, alluded to in his speech "The Drum Major Instinct." The impulse, he said, comes with a constructive and destructive side. Helping others, serving humanity—these are positive attributes of the instinct. However, the desires to be out front, to be first, to lead the parade—these are the negative parts of the drum major instinct. If not harnessed, Dr. King said, the instinct can lead to a sort of "snobbish exclusivism," where our egos dictate our actions.

Very few achievers want to then show off their warts by acknowledging the mistakes they've made along the way, much less put them in a book. I think that's unfortunate. Millions of people struggle with what it means to be successful, and the lesson they take away from successful folk who hide or deny their failures leads to an artificial construct of success. By "artificial" I mean the notion that people become successful without "success scars." Let me be clear: There is no success without failure. Period. And usually a lot of it.

I used to love Michael Jordan's "Failure" commercial for Nike. You might recall it:

> *I've missed more than 9,000 shots in my career*
> *I've lost almost 300 games*
> *26 times I've been trusted to take the game-winning shot*
> *. . . and missed*
> *I've failed over and over and over again in my life*
> *And that is why I succeed*

Powerful stuff.

The song "If I Can Help Somebody," written by Alma Bazel Androzzo, has motivated me over the years to share my personal failures in my speeches, on my television and radio programs, and with the young people we serve at the Tavis Smiley Foundation. Through my scars, I have been blessed to arrive at a place I never imagined. A place where that relentless teacher called experience now causes me to reflect on the nebulous concepts of *success* and *failure* in my own life.

In this book, I detail 20 of the most impactful lessons of my life. To be sure, I've failed plenty more than 20 times! But these events are the ones that caused me to wrestle with and ultimately embrace the true meaning of the exhortation by the Nobel Prize-winning playwright, novelist, and poet Samuel Beckett:

> *"Ever tried. Ever failed. No matter.*
> *Try again. Fail again. Fail better."*

Since I was 12, Dr. King has been my hero. As you progress through this book, you will better understand why I reserve such an esteemed place in my heart for this iconic servant-leader. What's not so well known is that I also deeply admire the courageous journey of Malcolm X. I respect his courage to wrestle with his own demons and his principled decision to sacrifice his anointed position with Elijah Muhammad and the Nation of Islam, the religion that rescued him from a life of crime and dissipation. The trek from Malcolm Little to Malcolm X to El-Hajj Malik El-Shabazz is a remarkable study in spiritual and political evolution and integrity.

In Malcolm's life, *failure* was an attribute. Consider his speech after returning from his pilgrimage to Mecca in 1964. As the public face of the Nation of Islam, he vehemently insisted that whites could play no role in the struggle for Black people's equality and independence. Whites, as far as Malcolm was concerned, were not part of his definition of brotherhood. That changed after his trip to the Holy Land.

*"I have never before seen sincere and true brotherhood practiced by all colors together, irrespective of their color. You may be shocked by these words coming from me. But on this pilgrimage, what I have seen, and experienced, has forced me to re-arrange much of my thought-patterns previously held, and to toss aside some of my previous conclusions. This was not too difficult for me. Despite my firm convictions, I have always been a man who tries to face facts, and to accept the reality of life as new experience and new knowledge unfolds it. I have always kept an open mind, which is necessary to the flexibility that must go hand in hand with every form of intelligent search for truth."*

Hopefully, this book channels Malcolm's commitment to personal growth. He didn't shrink from his failure to grasp the meaning of true brotherhood; he embraced it as a detour to new experiences and new knowledge.

In other words, he failed up.

Interestingly, it was my love for Martin that led me to Malcolm. Throughout history, pitting Black leaders against one another has been an effective maneuver. As a youngster, I wanted to know more about this guy Malcolm who was declared by the media and the man on the street to be the frightening antithesis of Martin. When I read the *Autobiography of Malcolm X*, I truly understood the worth and value of Malcolm's life and legacy. What's more, I discovered a connection with Malcolm that I did not find in Martin's life story.

The two men couldn't have started their lives in more diametrically different places. I really couldn't relate to Martin's upbringing because he was raised in a bourgeois, middle-class Black family. Malcolm's hardscrabble life, on the other hand, reflected my Mississippi and Indiana upbringing. His struggles with poverty, race, low self-esteem, family chaos, and trouble at school resonated with my life story at the time.

Not only did I grow to have an abiding love for Martin and Malcolm, I also wanted to emulate their powerful examples of courage, faith, resilience, and dedication to uplift our people.

These two men, my incontestable heroes, were both assassinated at the age of 39. My admiration and identification were so strong that I was convinced that I, too, would not live past the age of 39. Not that I was remotely putting myself on these icons' pedestals, no way. But sometimes, when the realities of your world become too harsh, an unconscious fatalism can overtake you and make you seek refuge in someone else's story as a way to make sense of your own.

But it wasn't just the far too brief lives of Martin and Malcolm that persuaded me that I would die young. There was another, perhaps even more influential factor that made the idea of my early demise seem an inevitable, stark reality.

Anybody familiar with the Pentecostal church—especially old-school Pentecostal church teachings—understands the ramifications of "hell and damnation" preached incessantly. "The world is going to end," "He's coming soon and if you're not living right, you're going to hell," "Armageddon is upon us—get right with God!" These were the messages that permeated the foundation of my childhood.

The combination of these thoughts—that my heroes were dead at the age of 39 and that the world's demise was imminent—had me living on the edge. I was scared to die and haunted by feelings that I would not have enough time to make the kind of societal contribution that I wanted to make. This underlying sense of urgency drove me to work hard, work fast, and succeed. Now!

Sure enough, as you will read in this book, I did work hard and I was blessed beyond measure.

By the age of 38, I had accomplished much: writing popular books, hosting national television and radio programs, being featured on the covers of magazines and newspapers, and so much more. I was even financially secure with a comfortable net worth.

Then I turned 39.

The fear that I would not make it to 40 began to overtake me. And what was worse is that I felt like I was a failure. Even though I was just one person—and a cracked vessel at that—I knew I hadn't done enough. For all that I had tried to accomplish, the problems in my community and my country and the world seemed so intractable. Poverty. Sickness. Crime. Racism. Environmental abuse. Child neglect. Educational inequities. War.

The night I turned 40, I was alone in a hotel room in Houston and had a major panic attack. The details of that night are so traumatic, forgive me for not wanting to relive them here. But shortly thereafter, I did share my nightmare in Houston with my abiding friend, Dr. Cornel West, over dinner.

Doc and I had talked many times before about my fear of dying young, so he understood the reason for the episode. But there was one part of my story he couldn't quite rationalize.

"How, at 40 years old, could you think that you are a failure?" he asked.

After I answered his question, Doc began to share with me his unique take on the matter of life and death:

"Tavis, the older I get, the more I think that there really is no such thing as penultimate success. I believe that every one of us essentially dies a failure."

Huh? Doc knew I was having trouble with his reasoning, so he pressed on:

"If one dies at 39, like Martin and Malcolm, or if one lives to be 139, you're not going to get it all done. There are going to be ideas you will never develop, projects you will never complete, conversations you will never have, people you will never meet, places you will never go, relationships you will never establish, forgiveness you will never receive, and books and speeches you will never write or deliver. We all die incomplete."

So, Doc added, "the central question becomes: How good is your failure?" With that, he dropped the Beckett quote on me:

*"Ever tried. Ever failed. No matter.*
*Try again. Fail again. Fail better."*

Doc was right. Ultimately, life is about failing better. Every day you wake up, you get another chance to get it right, to come up from failure, to fail up.

In working with young people through our foundation, I no longer use the phrase *just do your best*. If what you give the world is your best, then how do you get better?

The conversation with Dr. West freed me because it gave me a different perspective on the true meaning and the real value of failure.

Beckett's quote has become one of my favorites. I share it with young or old, Black or white, whenever I have the opportunity. Motivational speaker Les Brown says, "When life knocks you down, try to land on your back. Because if you can look up, you can get up."

Failure is an inevitable part of the human journey. *Fail up* is the trampoline needed when you're down. When you take the time to learn your lessons, when you use those lessons as stepping-stones to climb even higher than you were before, you transcend failure—you "fail up."

As I celebrate 20 years as a broadcaster, now is the time to show my scars. I hope the 20 lessons presented in the following chapters will offer you a new way to think about your failures.

I'm a witness. You *can* fail up.

© Courtesy of the Tavis Smiley Collection

© Courtesy of the Tavis Smiley Collection

# CHAPTER 1

# BEFORE HONOR COMES HUMILITY

*"When you are as great as I am
it's hard to be humble."*

— MUHAMMAD ALI

One of my fondest adolescent memories was sitting in front of my family's black-and-white, floor-model television with my Dad watching the fights broadcast on ABC Sports hosted by Howard Cosell. We watched one heavyweight in particular—Muhammad Ali. My Dad, like a whole lot of Black men back then, was a huge Ali fan. Eventually, his hero became my hero, and I loved watching those fights with him.

There was something about Ali that attracted me even more than his ability to dance, shuffle, and knock you out. An articulate and braggadocious talker, Ali predicted the outcome of his fights in rhyme: "You're going down in the third round!" Mostly, I loved Ali because he wasn't afraid of white folk. Be it defending his religion or his stance against the Vietnam War, he used his mind and his mouth to whip opponents inside and outside the ring.

Imagine Ali's impact on a Black child who constantly felt like an outsider. The only time I saw Black folk, other than my family, was when we attended an all-Black church some 30 miles away from our home. As I detailed in my memoir, *What I Know For Sure*, I was raised in Indiana, lived in an all-white trailer park, and attended a virtually all-white school.

There were ten kids and three adults living in a double-wide trailer. Money was tighter than tight. It wasn't unusual for the Smiley children to wear hand-me-down clothes or shoes with cardboard tucked inside the soles to cover holes. Neighborhood white kids didn't hesitate to point out that my family was poorer, bigger, and blacker than theirs.

I developed a deep sense of class- and race-based inferiority.

But that was before I came under the spell of Muhammad Ali.

I convinced myself that Ali and I shared similar traits. I was smarter than most of my classmates, I had an excellent memory, and I could out-talk anybody. If Ali could challenge white people with his mind and his mouth, so could I.

I began to check classmates with my quickness—correcting them if they were wrong, arguing with them if they thought they were right, and placing bets to prove that I could articulate faster, more eloquently, and more accurately than they could.

Substituting feelings of inferiority with intellectual superiority helped me verbally knock out contenders left and right. And, for awhile, it felt great. Problem was, during my Ali phase, I started getting into physical fights and trouble with teachers at school. The worst part—nobody liked me.

Because of my mind and mouth, I could make no friends.

## The Arrogance of Youth

If you study Ali's life, particularly when he was younger, you'll understand why I was having trouble making friends in school. Although I wasn't using derogatory put-downs, my desire to verbally knock out my challengers and to impress with lightning-fast wit was perceived as arrogance. My peers had no idea I was fighting an inner battle against race and poverty-based low self-esteem. They didn't know I was trying to prove that I was "the greatest" orator for my own survival.

As you progress through this book, you'll note some important lessons I learned due to my ill-timed or unwise use of words. But, back in the mid-1970s, I was too caught up in pubescent adulation of Ali's razzle-dazzle to give much thought to the damage his poetic slings and barbs might have wrought on his opponents.

I was born seven months after Ali defeated ex-con and knockout expert Sonny Liston in 1964. I was just a baby when, after the first Liston fight, Ali announced to the world that he had become a member of the Nation of Islam and had changed his name from Cassius Clay to Muhammad Ali. Years later, at the age of 11, I was too young to really comprehend the injustices or ramifications of the Vietnam War.

Yet somehow, these events were all part of the magical lore of the quick-footed boxer my father adored.

Through his stories, I learned that Ali had been exiled from boxing after refusing to fight in the war. My father's excitement was contagious when Ali came back to the ring in 1970. Together, we celebrated his triumphs over Jerry Quarry, Oscar Bonavena, Ken Norton, and Joe Frazier in the early 1970s. My father and I were side by side when Ali defied all odds and floored the one-punch wonder George Foreman in 1974. And, of course, we had to watch when two of the best fighters of all time—Ali and Frazier—fought for the third time. To this day, the "Thrilla in Manila" fight stands as one of the greatest heavyweight bouts in boxing history.

It's been reported that 21 years after that infamous match, Joe Frazier still bore the scars of Ali's verbal abuse.

"Before we fought, the words hurt more than the punches," Frazier told author Thomas Hauser for Ali's biography, *Muhammad Ali: His Life and Times.*

Frazier—a hard-hitting, take-no-prisoners Philadelphia brawler born in segregated Beaufort, South Carolina—didn't deserve the dishonor heaped on him by Ali:

"Frazier is so ugly that he should donate his face to the U.S. Bureau of Wildlife."

"It's gonna be a thrilla, and a chilla, and a killa, when I get the Gorilla in Manila."

That last riff was emphasized with a tiny gorilla doll Ali sometimes carried with him that was supposed to represent Frazier. Although many whites hoped Frazier would give Ali his comeuppance, "Smokin' Joe" did not fit the criteria of the white man's champion. Thus Ali's taunts were like unnecessary, below-the-belt blows. Frazier by no means deserved to be called a "gorilla" or an "Uncle Tom."

Time seems to have given Frazier the perspective to move past the pain Ali's words caused. "You have to throw that stick out of the window," he told *Sports Illustrated* writer Matthew Syed in 2005. "Do not forget," Frazier added, "we needed each other to produce some of the greatest fights of all time."

The national desire to have someone finally shut him up and the millions that could be made in the process helped Ali regain his license, get back in the ring, and dominate the game. Throughout his career, Muhammad Ali used his mouth and in-your-face tactics to force his way back into boxing. I think he was also forcing himself to prove that he could overcome obstacles that no other boxer had ever had to contend with.

In a 2001 one-on-one interview for *O* magazine, Oprah Winfrey touched on the topic. During the interview, she reminded Ali that Black and white people considered him the underdog and had bet against him before his fight with Liston.

"Were you scared?" Winfrey asked.

"I was scared to death. Before that fight, I did so much predicting and talked so much that I had to win," Ali answered.

It's important to note that Ali was a strapping 22-year-old when he fought Liston. He was scared, but his boasting and swagger before and after that fight speak to the arrogance of youth or, to be more accurate, the perception of "arrogance" attached to the audacious actions of young folk.

There's a reason young people traditionally fuel the tsunami of change in this world. Joan of Arc led French armies to several major victories before she was executed at the age of 19; journalist, publisher, and civil rights activist, Ida B. Wells-Barnett was only 25 when she began writing articles that challenged and chronicled racial injustice in the United States; Dr. Martin Luther King, Jr. was 26 when he was selected to lead the Montgomery Bus Boycott; Bill Gates was 19 when he founded Microsoft Corp. in 1974; Steve Jobs and Steve Wozniak were 21 and 25, respectively, when they began selling the Apple-1 in 1976; Mark Zuckerberg was 19 when he launched the social networking site Facebook® in 2004.

Young people have the courage to challenge the status quo. They have the energy and natural inclination to prove something to themselves and to the world. Rebellion has always fermented on college campuses around the world because young people are willing to disrupt, offend, and bear the consequences of their convictions just to ensure that their voices are heard and their ideas and passions are respected.

Yet, as Dr. King emphasized in his "Drum Major" sermon, there's a double-edged reality that's implicit in youthful attempts to prove themselves. In an effort to fight for a cause, uphold an absolute right, or stand on principle, sometimes reckless arrogance fueled by a lack of experience or immaturity can hurt or offend people unnecessarily.

An Arabian proverb sums it up nicely: *"Arrogance diminishes wisdom."*

In countless interviews since retiring from boxing, Ali has insisted that he was never the man at home people saw on television or in the boxing ring. The name-calling and put-downs of his opponents were only ways to promote fights, he said. Mike Marqusee, author of *Redemption Song: Muhammad Ali and the Spirit of the Sixties*, described Ali as a "modest man." After observing Ali away from the public, Marqusee pondered, "Could it be that the most notorious boaster in the history of sport was, at the bottom of it all, a humble man?"

Personally, I like to think of Ali as a humble man of great conviction who, on occasion, let his youthful passion override his ability to show compassion.

Today, I can see how Ali's verbal jabs and stinging slights could have devastated boxers like Frazier. But, as an insecure boy trying to carve a niche for himself in an awkward and seemingly unfriendly environment, Ali was "The Man."

It took a wise and compassionate woman to pull me off a reckless path.

## It's Hard to Be Humble . . .

Mama quickly noticed my growing ego problem. "Tavis," she cautioned, "you don't have to run around trying to prove how smart and bright you are. Stop all that!"

Her warnings weren't exactly having an immediate effect.

One day, after Mama and Dad returned from a brief weekend getaway, she passed out gifts to all my siblings but me. She asked me to stay behind as she shooed my brothers and sisters outside. We sat together at the big family kitchen table.

"I got you something," she said, holding up a small, blond, wooden pencil holder. Under the little holes drilled in its top, I noticed a black laminated inscription:

> "It's hard to be humble when
> you're as great as I am."

Focusing on the last four words, the Ali in me exclaimed: "Yeah!"

"Read it again," Mama responded.

I did, again and again, apparently not quite getting it.

Mama, being more direct, insisted that I read only the first part:

> *"It's hard to be humble . . .*
> *It's hard to be humble . . ."*

Slowly, it dawned on me that she wasn't exactly paying me a compliment.

"Tavis, sweetie," she continued, "you are so lovable but you're so not likable. You're not likable because you're too brash, too in people's faces, too much of a smart aleck. You walk around posturing your greatness. You have a humility problem, baby, and we have to fix this problem right now."

That's when she pulled out her Bible and hit me with Proverbs 27:2:

> *"Let another man praise thee,*
> *and not thine own mouth;*
> *a stranger, and not thine own lips."*

"Do you know what that means?" Mama asked, not pausing for my answer. "It means you don't want to be exalting yourself and patting yourself on the back. A leader doesn't exalt himself; a true leader is exalted by the people.

"You're not giving people any room to celebrate you, to revel in your accomplishments; you're telling them before they ever get a chance."

Not content with the Biblical lesson, Mama suggested an experiment:

"Tavis, for just one week, I want you to not say anything about yourself—don't reference yourself at all. You just do what you do, without bragging about it for a whole week, and I can almost guarantee you that somebody, somewhere, is going to recognize your contribution."

Following her directions and trying the experiment would result in my feeling much better about myself "on the inside," Mama promised.

"Whatever feelings you get from running your mouth and bragging are going to pale to what it feels like when somebody else praises you."

So, for the next few days, I avoided verbal beat-downs and boasting about myself. One day, after reciting the entire lineup of the Cincinnati Reds, including their current batting averages, I purposely chose not to challenge my classmates to best me, nor did I brag about what I had just done. I simply sat down.

Sure enough, a few impressed classmates complimented my "amazing" memory.

I couldn't wait to get off the school bus, run home, and tell Mama about my experience. She smiled and cried at the same time.

"That's what I was trying to tell you, baby. Remember that feeling for as long as you live because the more you achieve and succeed, the more you'll discover how difficult it will be to remain humble. Always remember, before honor comes humility."

# Humility—the Flip Side of Arrogance

*"I think the reason I have come as far as I have
stems from insecurity . . . I'm sure there are lots of
people in the business—even in politics—and the CEOs
of enormous companies, who get there because
insecurity pushes you. I sometimes think the brasher
the celebrity or the artist, the more
insecure they are."*

—MICHAEL BUBLÉ

Canadian crooner Michael Bublé's disclosure struck a chord with me. Not only have I met some of those notables he describes; I, too, once shouldered the burden of insecurity—feeling *less than, not good enough.* The false fronts of bravado and braggadocio were used to mask those insecurities. If not for a mother's stubborn love and a small, wooden pencil box, there's no telling how many friends or opportunities I might have lost.

The lesson learned was one of humility. And I thank God I "got it" at an early age. You see, we live in a society where broken people desperately seek external validations to feel worthy. The whole motivation behind the "buy, buy, buy," "gotta have, gotta have" mentality is an attempt to purchase status and stature. Young people, lacking confidence, are bamboozled into believing that the "real life" shown on many of the reality TV programs is loud, brash, obnoxious, and self-gratifying.

The media have created an inaccurate image of a successful business person as someone who is self-centered and materialistic, says John M. Thompson III, executive director of career services at Texas Christian University. As a result, Thompson suggests, many young entrepreneurs approach their careers from an arrogant, what's-in-it-for-me perspective, when "the business world does not like arrogance."

Arrogance, the flip side of humility, is celebrated in the media, movies, and politics. It is the spark that leads to chest-thumping, unilateral offenses, and the downfall of politicians or Wall Street types who egotistically believe they are beyond reproof. People who are decent and courteous during face-to-face encounters exhibit opposite personas in the ever-expanding world of faceless Internet communication.

In the study "Arrogance: A Formula for Failure," Stan Silverman, dean of The University of Akron's Summit College and co-author of the study, notes the strong connection among arrogance, poor job performance, and negativity on the job.

Silverman and his colleagues developed the Workplace Arrogance Scale (WARS) to obtain empirical data that verified or negated the alleged negative relationship between arrogance and job performance. Among other findings, the study concluded that the more arrogant a person is, the more self-centered and the less agreeable he or she is likely to be. Further, it found arrogance can have significant negative effects on an organization's morale and profitability.

"There might be a competitive advantage in curtailing arrogant behavior in organizations and encouraging positive behaviors such as humility," Silverman adds.

If arrogance is the disease, then humility is the cure. If we want to create a balance where our passions don't elicit accusations of arrogance, then we must strive for abundant doses of humility. This trait silences the ego's chatter and helps fill our lives and our world with positive, progressive, and holistic energy.

Ali once said, "A man who views the world the same at fifty as he did at twenty has wasted thirty years of his life."

Humility seems to be the ingredient that spared Ali a wasted life. Long after he'd left the boxing world, a reporter from Soundvision, an Islamic Website, asked Ali how he balanced his "supreme confidence" with the humility he's supposed to strive for as a Muslim.

"Allah is the Greatest. I'm just the greatest boxer," Ali replied.

It's mostly insecure people who boast about their status and stature. Sometimes, such self-absorption slides into the realm of narcissism.

I have long since proven to folks inside and outside my old neighborhood what I'm capable of, what God has given me. Still, certain insecurities remain, and I don't think I'm unlike other high-profile people. There's always that struggle within yourself to prove yourself.

To find balance, feel free to use Mama's experiment. Before honoring yourself, try humility.

Remember, Ali's self-proclamation didn't make him great. Standing up for right made Ali "The Greatest." History bore witness to the truth of his personal convictions.

After all these years, it still feels better when somebody else acknowledges me instead of me acknowledging myself. As I was working on this book, *USA Today* ran a story listing the top TV shows that could help viewers expand their vocabularies. *Tavis Smiley* on PBS was among the writer's top five personal picks.

Having *USA Today* tell folks to "watch the *Tavis Smiley* show if you want to elevate your vocabulary" was much better than my taking out an ad to say: "Watch the *Tavis Smiley* show if you want to be smarter!"

Finding organic ways to boost our confidence is always good. But you can be confident without being cocky. Focusing, reaching, and praying for humility will help us achieve balance.

Nevertheless, my conviction and passions have sometimes been misconstrued. The people that label me "arrogant" have no idea how committed I am to remembering the lesson of humility. If it even appeared that I had become too full of myself, believe me, a matriarch from Kokomo,

Indiana wouldn't hesitate to call and remind me to go read the inscription on the pencil box I still have in my home.

Still, I am not perfect. So every day I recite my "humility prayer":

"Lord, whatever you do, help me to remain humble. Don't ever let me get to a point where I'm unnecessarily praising myself."

The prayer gives me balance. It reminds me of a loving mother's sage advice:

"Before honor comes humility."

> ## TAVIS'S TAKEAWAY:
>
> Stay humble
> or stumble.

© Courtesy of the Tavis Smiley Collection

# CHAPTER 2

# CHEATERS
# NEVER WIN

I had to whisper "Amen!"

On September 10, 2010, columnist George Will, economist Paul Krugman, ABC News political director Amy Walter, and I were waiting our turn to go on the air and discuss politics with the host of ABC's *This Week with Christiane Amanpour.*

There was a lot of chatter in the Green Room that day. My attention, however, was diverted to the conversation between Amanpour and the guest who preceded us—French Finance Minister Christine Lagarde.

"You were a former CEO; do you think women have a different way of approaching business or approaching the public sphere?" Amanpour asked the finance minister.

"Yes . . . I think we inject less libido, less testosterone into the equation," Lagarde responded. "It helps in the sense that we don't necessarily project our own egos into cutting a deal, making our point across . . . convincing people, reducing them to a partner that has lost in the process."

Lagarde admitted to over-generalizing. She said that there are indeed women who operate exactly like men. But, she added, ". . . I honestly believe that there are a majority of women in such positions that approach power, decision-making processes, and other people in business relationships in a slightly different manner."

Immediately, Lagarde's words took me back to a precarious time when my career could have ended before it even began. As a college student, I made a foolish, potentially disastrous mistake that could have put me behind bars and destroyed my public ambitions forever. It was a woman—a very powerful woman—who resisted the advice of a male subordinate who wanted to crucify me for my recklessness.

This woman of authority, who handled a delicate situation in a "slightly different manner" than a man, profoundly impacted my life. It is because of her, in part, that I rely on the instincts of women. My company was started with a brilliant woman and, to this day, women run the majority of my enterprises. The levels of professional excellence, emotional intelligence, and wisdom they bring into my universe are invaluable.

I don't know why Amanpour seguéd from the topic of European finance to the question about women in power. To me, it was but another divine reminder—a flashback to a lesson learned about benevolence, tough love, the blessings inherent with a second chance, and, most importantly, the value of personal integrity and ethics.

And so, I just had to say "Amen!"

## Cheater

The off-campus shooting of Denver Smith on September 12, 1983, rocked the worlds of students and faculty members at Indiana University in Bloomington. Denver—a football star, husband, father to a brand-new baby girl, and my kindhearted friend—was shot in the back four times by local police officers. Police spokesmen told reporters that Smith, 24 at the time, was acting "erratically and deranged." He was scuffling with officers when they shot him in the back.

This incident was the first encounter that I, a kid from the small town of Kokomo, Indiana, had with what many of us on campus perceived as racism and prejudice. As a sophomore and the highest-ranking Black person in student government, I was often quoted in the media denouncing what had happened to Denver.

The case took its legal route but, in the process, Bloomington Mayor Tomilea Allison assembled a blue-ribbon commission, the Bloomington Community Progress Council. The group was charged with developing an agenda that would advance the city socially, culturally, and economically. It also recommended community outreach efforts that might, hopefully, prevent another high-profile incident like the one that robbed Denver Smith of his life.

Our initial introduction—me, as an angry advocate for police accountability, and Mayor Allison, as the city's top official and defender of all things city-related—was somewhat antagonistic. Still, she took a liking to me and gave me the opportunity to intern for her.

The biggest part of my job was to serve as the mayor's liaison to the prestigious community progress council. Imagine the opportunity: There I was—a 20-year-old pre-law/public policy major with a small office in the mayor's suite. Not only was I studying it at school, I was also helping to shape public policy every day.

It was beyond cool.

Mayor Allison trusted me implicitly, so much so that I was allowed to fill out my own time card. To this day, if you asked what motivated me to start padding my time sheet, I don't know that I can offer an honest answer. It began almost imperceptibly. If I worked six hours, I'd put down eight. If I worked eight, I'd put down ten.

I justified my actions by rationalizing that I wasn't really doing anything *that* bad. They only paid me minimum wage—a meager amount for the huge investment of my time and energy on the mayor's project. Besides, I needed the extra cash. I was the first person on either my mother or father's side of the family to ever go to college. The debate team and trying to keep my grades up dominated my busy schedule. I could not let the lack of money jeopardize my success. *Survival* was the excuse I leaned on to blot everything my parents and my church had taught me about honesty and trust.

The trust the mayor had in me was not shared by other members of her staff. One day, I was told to report to the office of the deputy mayor, a no-nonsense man who wasn't exactly enthralled with the mayor's choice for community liaison.

The deputy mayor laid out undeniable evidence that proved I had been cheating on my time sheets. I was busted. He immediately checked off the procedure he'd recommend to the mayor—notify the police, have me arrested, fire me, and publicly humiliate me for my actions.

What?! Until that moment, I had never connected padding a few hours here and there with the police, being arrested, or going to jail! At first I was just humiliated. I had betrayed everything I had learned in life about "truth, truth, and more truth." But the more the deputy mayor talked, the quicker my humiliation escalated to fear of going to jail.

I dreaded with all my heart meeting with Mayor Allison the following day. The solemn look in her eyes alone reduced me to Jell-O®.

"Tavis, you have disappointed me. I never expected this from you," the mayor said. She never expected me to be a "fabricator, a cheater, a thief." Without hesitating for a response, she added that I wasn't just a "thief," I was the "worst kind of thief" because I stole "the people's money."

In my meeting with the deputy mayor, there was humiliation but no emotion. I didn't shed a tear. Mayor Allison had me at "disappointed," but when she hit me with the cold hard fact that

I had stolen from taxpayers, that I had violated the people's trust
... well, as my grandfather used to say, "I gave up all kinda water."

## Admonish but Affirm

Mayor Allison, who is white, could have chosen a path taken
by so many people of authority with little tolerance for wayward
Black youth. She could have had me locked up and forever locked
out of a promising career. Instead, she did something most people in her position probably never would have considered. She
looked across her desk at a sniffling, broken, and humiliated
Black college student and decided to affirm his value.

"Tavis, when I first met you and saw how you articulated
and expressed yourself and organized students, I had such
high hopes for you," the mayor began. "No," she stopped herself, "let me rephrase that. I don't want to say 'had.' I *have* high
hopes for you. I know how successful you can be—and I'm not
just talking about what you have to offer Black people. You
have so much to offer the American people."

Wow! Talk about a teachable moment. Here I am thinking
I'm on the verge of being arrested, and this woman not only
reprimands me but takes the time to affirm me as well.

Fast-forward some 25 years and the mayor's lesson stays
with me. When it's necessary to enforce a serious course correction among my employees, I try to affirm them as well.
Over and over again, starting with Mayor Allison, I've been

reminded that you can correct and even reprimand somebody, but, at the same time, you can also affirm that person. If you are in a position of power, you can also offer a second chance. This simple but powerful act gives the accused a chance to not only learn from the transgression, but it also provides the incentive to never risk losing that respected person's trust again. At least it did for me.

Ignoring the advice of her deputy, Mayor Allison laid out, in specific detail, how I would rectify my situation. She expected me to go over all my time sheets and give her the best estimate of what I stole from the taxpayers.

"I'm trusting that you're going to do it with every bit of honesty you have in your body," she said. "And when we figure it out, we're going to calculate what it is in hours, and you're going to work off those hours. You're going to give this time back to the city. In essence, by the end of the day, you will not have stolen from the city."

And that's exactly what I did—calculated those hours to the minute and worked all of them off—and then some. When I paid back the money, there was no patting me on the back. Mayor Allison simply acknowledged that I had lived up to her expectations.

And that was more than good enough for me.

After she described how I would pay the city back, the mayor added a final caveat:

"Tavis, I think you're going to learn a lesson from this."

She was more than right. I learned a life lesson I'll never forget.

## A Culture of Cheaters

Today's headlines are filled with news of cheaters: Former investment adviser Bernard "Bernie" Madoff, sentenced to 150 years in prison for bilking investors out of billions through a massive Ponzi scheme; the collective black eye Major League Baseball received after numerous media reports exposed the extent of performance-enhancing steroid use; city officials in Bell, a small southern California town, arrested and charged with misappropriating more than $5 million in city money for their personal use.

One of the reasons I'm such a stickler for accountability is because I know what it means to violate the public trust. Although I list theft of taxpayer money among the most egregious offenses, I recognize the common denominator among ripping off voters, stealing from investors, and using steroids—they are all acts of betrayal. Just as I had disappointed Mayor Allison and the citizens of Bloomington, these individuals betrayed dozens, hundreds, even thousands who trusted and respected them.

These examples are but a few high-profile cases of cheating. Society is filled with so many other more pedestrian examples: executives who fudge their educational credentials or work records on résumés just to appear more experienced and successful; students who plagiarize work from the Internet for better grades; employees who play computer games or chat online or on cell phones while on the company's dime.

We rationalize these acts, tell ourselves it's a temporary means to an end, or it's really no big deal. In actuality, it is. Be it padding our résumés or time sheets, using company computers for personal reasons, or stealing pens or paper towels from work, it reinforces a culture of disrespect and destroys the meaning of personal integrity.

I remember a Slate.com article I read in 2002 about a whole slew of executives caught that year lying about their educational achievements. These men represented companies like Bausch & Lomb, Veritas Software, and Salomon Smith Barney. According to William Baker, a contributor for the CBS Interactive Business Network, "Stretching in résumés—fiddling with dates of employment to hide long layoffs; inflating the magnitude of your job responsibilities—is prevalent. A common figure thrown about in studies and by human resources professionals is that 40 percent of résumés are not exactly on the level."

What does all this mean? Well, it means "the little white lies"—the fudging and skimming and skirting of responsibilities—are now part of our work culture. It means there are thousands, maybe millions, of workers and executives out there paralyzed with fear, afraid their secrets—large or small—will be exposed or their careers will be ruined. It means we live in a society dominated by cheaters.

My career started on the inside of the body politic working as a public servant. Now, I'm on the outside but still working for the public—with public TV and radio programs. In college, I learned to regard the public's trust and its money seriously. In media, it's the same; nothing is more valuable or sacred than the public trust. Whether I'm on TV or radio, delivering a speech, or conducting an interview—integrity is as important to me now as it was when Mayor Allison taught me that tough-love lesson in integrity years ago. From that day forward, I vowed never to disregard, misuse, or violate the public's trust.

Likewise, wherever you work, whatever you do, remember: Integrity and trust are so terribly important—not only for your company, but for you, your family, and our society as well.

## Accept Responsibility, Make Amends, and Recover

Because of one stupid, desperate act, everything had exploded in the young college student's world. Keisha didn't know if she'd be heading back to school to start her junior year or not. Her mother and father were going through a bitter divorce. The thought of depleting more of her mother's scarce resources troubled her deeply. She had secured a summer job at a clothing store but hadn't earned nearly enough to survive another semester.

One day, when no one was looking, she stole a few hundred dollars from the store's cash register. As it turns out, someone *was* looking. The police were called. The honors student who had never committed a crime in her life was arrested. Although her mother made sure the store was reimbursed, she feared charges would be filed against her daughter.

Keisha's mother was an acquaintance of mine. She had read my memoir and recalled my experience with Mayor Allison.

"You were a college student around the same age when you almost lost your way," she said. The failure had taken a heavy toll on both mother and child. "Will you please talk to her, Tavis?"

When Keisha and I met, I saw a female version of my younger self. Her shame was palpable. At first, she had trouble even looking me in the eyes. She didn't need me to chastise her. Everybody in her circle had already done that.

She needed clear-eyed support, direction, and affirmation as well.

I sat with Keisha and explained that I'd heard lots of good things about her academic achievement and potential. Then I shared my failure and what I had to do to truly learn my lesson. I explained why saying *I'm sorry* isn't enough. What I had learned from the mayor was that my betrayal of trust not only required an apology; it also required making amends. *Sorry* is a convenient word, but *making amends* means admitting that you were wrong and making a change. There was a price to pay for failing to maintain her integrity, I said, but hopefully she had learned that a failure or falling down is irreversible only when we fail to take responsibility for our actions and correct our behavior.

Let's compare the stories of New York Congressman Charles Rangel, former House Majority leader Tom DeLay, and Philadelphia Eagles quarterback Michael Vick. The 11 counts the House Ethics Committee issued against Rangel in 2010 charging him with violating its rules were pretty damning. Rangel protested, saying that his actions didn't rise to the level of House censure, which is the strongest punishment short of outright expulsion. Considering some of the personal misdeeds of Members of Congress within the past 20 years, Rep. Rangel makes a valid point. Although his lawyers insisted that he had not intentionally violated any laws and had not misused his office for personal financial gain, the legendary Congressman is now recorded in history as someone who was censured after violating House ethics, and whose detractors judged him as someone who never accepted full responsibility for his actions.

Tom DeLay faces a similar designation. In January 2011, the once-bulletproof Texan was sentenced to three years in prison for illegally plotting to channel corporate contributions to Texas legislative candidates. Even after his sentencing, DeLay maintained his innocence based on the defense that he was simply doing what "everybody was doing" and that he was the victim of political persecution. The responsibility-dodging DeLay has vowed to appeal the verdict.

Michael Vick, on the other hand, claimed his crime and seems to be on an admirable road to redemption. In July 2007, his football career with the Atlanta Falcons came to a screeching halt. After he was indicted for running a dog-fighting operation, Vick was suspended by the NFL without pay and lost all his well-paying endorsement deals. Months before his sentencing, Vick went before the media and apologized to the NFL, the Atlanta Falcons, and his fans for "using bad judgment and making bad decisions.

"I will redeem myself. I have to."

An article in the December 27, 2010, edition of *The Christian Science Monitor* discussed Vick's "rehabilitation both as a person and a football player" and his "fairy tale year" in football after serving 18 months in federal prison. According to the article, Vick credits his sentencing and time in prison with making him a better player:

"Arguably the best running quarterback in the history of the NFL, Vick has now added patience and better passing to his repertoire, making him a complete pro quarterback for the first time in his career."

It's important to note that someone with power gave Vick a second chance. As the newspaper article pointed out, there was "only tepid interest among NFL teams" when Vick was released. He was signed by the Eagles in 2009 as a backup starting quarterback. When Kevin Kolb was named the Eagles's starting quarterback, Vick did not complain and showed unequivocal support for the young player. When Kolb was injured early in the 2010 season, Vick got the chance to show what he could do. According to the article, "His performances have turned the Eagles from a team scrapping to make the playoffs into a legitimate threat to reach the Super Bowl."

Although Vick and the Eagles didn't make it to the Super Bowl in 2011, as I was writing this chapter, it was reported that Vick had been named starting quarterback for the NFL Pro Bowl game in Honolulu. His resurgence would have never been as widely celebrated had he not had the courage to admit his misdeeds and the integrity to work toward redemption.

# When You Fall Prey to Human Failing

What I tried to share with Keisha was the value of integrity. Staying on an honorable path means that you work to identify the temptations and weaknesses and always strive to "catch yourself" before they lead you into difficult situations. I wanted her to understand that, if she does fall prey to human failings, it is so important to take personal responsibility, acknowledge the error, accept the punishment, and make amends to rectify the mistake. You can't fail up if you cast yourself as a victim or try to rationalize your behavior with a myriad of excuses.

I asked Keisha to vow to herself that she would not let a thoughtless act turn into a definition of her character. I reminded her of her innate worth and assured her that if she employed the moral compass that her mother had instilled in her and remained true to her values, she would indeed overcome this *failure* to be all that she really was.

Thanks to a lesson learned from a powerful woman and the blessing of a second chance, I was able to confidently leave Keisha with an empowering message:

"While there's nothing honorable about trying to get ahead in life by cheating, there's almost nothing in life from which you cannot recover," especially if you have help.

This part applies to those who encounter someone like a young Tavis, a Keisha, or a Michael Vick. When you discipline, it isn't necessary to destroy. You have the power to reprimand, affirm, and allow individuals to redeem themselves. I believe in redemption and resurrection in both the spiritual and the philosophical senses. Although I'm not much for third, fourth, or fifth chances, I have embraced the value of extending the second chance.

Shortly before writing this chapter, I had to call an emergency meeting with three employees who had made some very bad decisions that cost the company serious money. Frankly, I laid it on the line. If it happened again, I said, they'd all lose their jobs. But in that same conversation, I made sure that they knew that I valued them, trusted them implicitly, and appreciated everything they had done to help grow our enterprise. Because of that affirming second chance, the employees doubled their efforts to show me that my decision not to fire them was the best decision I could have ever made.

Remember, when Mayor Allison gave me the opportunity to pay back all the money I owed the city, she said, "Tavis, I think you're going to learn a lesson from this."

She was right. I learned that cheaters never win. I also learned that some cheaters deserve a second chance. Sometimes redemptive second chances allow you to fail up.

## TAVIS'S TAKEAWAY:

There's nothing that you can't recover from—with help.

© Courtesy of the Tavis Smiley Collection

# CHAPTER 3

# DON'T DO ME NO FAVORS

Although I make my living on television, I'm no expert on the formula that makes a particular show a hit or miss with its audience. However, there was one HBO series that I figured out pretty quickly—*Entourage*. It's about four childhood friends from Queens transplanted to Hollywood via the success of their curly-headed leader, Vincent Chase (actor Adrian Grenier). The testosterone-heavy show, loosely based on the life of celebrity Mark Wahlberg, revolves around the gang's party-hopping, woman-chasing, star-gazing, and movie-making adventures.

I understand the appeal. The entourage has the hookup, thanks to Vince's sudden ascent to A-list status. And, as we all know, everybody wants the hookup! Inside or outside Hollywood, everybody wishes they had a go-to person, a powerful friend who can grant magic-wand-like favors and provide instant access to big-name concerts, sporting events, chic night clubs, jaunts with the rich and famous, or the right connections to help secure a sensational, high-paying job or other opportunities.

I know I did. When this Kokomo kid arrived in LA in 1985, I was instantly hypnotized by the city's glitz and glamour and eagerly anticipated running with the big dogs. I didn't have a "Vince." But I did have Jim Brown, the best player to ever bulldoze his way up and down a football field.

Through a failure I experienced with Jim, I learned an invaluable lesson about the real price tag of the *favor* game.

## A Lesson in Tinseltown

Earlier that year, I met Jim by way of Chi, my college roommate. We had gone to LA to attend a national convention of student leaders. Tamara, Chi's cousin, was Jim's friend. After driving us to his home in Hollywood Hills, Tamara introduced me to the pro football Hall-of-Famer-turned-actor-turned-activist, who was in his kitchen engaged in a serious game of backgammon (a game he loves). After Tamara told him I was a promising student leader, Jim said, to my delight: "Great. We need a couple more young men like you."

Jim then introduced me to his backgammon buddy, George Hughley, a former Washington Redskins football player. The chance meeting was a testament to a favorite saying of my grandmother, "Big Mama": "That's the kind of God we serve!"

Once I landed in LA, I started formulating a plan to stay. The idea that I could do another internship, this time with LA Mayor Tom Bradley, was percolating in my head. Meeting George was a blessing. Not only was he incredibly helpful, he had also worked for Mayor Bradley.

The next day, George drove me to City Hall. I was introduced to several members of the mayor's staff, including Craig Lawson, the official in charge of internships. Craig told me to write a letter when I got back to school, and he'd give my internship request every consideration.

After more than nine months of writing weekly letters, making numerous phone calls, and enduring two frustrating flights back to LA to plead my case, I eventually received a phone call from the mayor's office. My perseverance had paid off: The mayor invited me back to Los Angeles to intern for him.

Jim graciously agreed to let me stay with him until I got settled. So there I was, my first few weeks in California, crashing in the guest house of one of the most well-known celebrities in all of Hollywood. I spent a good month living the high-life, gawking and greeting visiting celebrities and notables I'd seen only on TV, movie screens, and magazine covers. With the kind of raging ambition I had, it was impossible for me to avoid greedily lapping up as much of Jim's world as I possibly could.

He was accommodating, making sure I was comfortable in his home and, on occasion, offering me tickets to concerts and other events. It was his kindness combined with my star-struck naïveté that began to fuel my habit of asking for things before my host even offered. With parrot-like persistence, I'd ask: "Jim, can I go here . . . Jim, can I go there . . . Can I do this, Jim . . . Can I . . . Can I . . . Jim, Jim, Jim?"

Not known for suffering fools gladly, Jim had apparently grown weary of my entreaties. One day, I approached him while he was playing his favorite game poolside with a few friends. I can't recall his exact words, but I do remember Jim's steely "I'm-about-to-go-off" glare.

"Why are you always begging so much?"

Right in front of his amused backgammon buddies, Big Jim laid me out:

"Listen, I don't ask people for anything. The reason I don't is because I don't want to owe. Every time I ask somebody for something, you can rest assured they're going to ask me for something later. And I don't want to spend my life returning favors.

"If somebody gives me something, that's one thing—because I'm Jim Brown, people do give me stuff. But I don't go around asking," Jim continued. "If I don't do it for myself, I sho' ain't gonna be returning no favors for you. So just stop asking me!"

Whoa!

Standing there, a thoroughly humiliated 20-year-old, I made two vows to myself:

> #1: Never ask Jim Brown for anything again, ever!
> #2: Get the heck out of Big Jim's house!

It took my moving out and time for my adolescent ego to heal, but eventually, I reached the obvious conclusion that Jim was a straight shooter who told me exactly what I most needed to hear. Even though I didn't appreciate the verbal smack-down, in my grown-up, professional life, I have come to respect Jim's mantra: "Don't do me no favors!"

## "Oh No, What Do They Want Now?"

As I've had to hustle, scratch, and finesse my way through life, I've come to realize just how right Big Jim was. Every time I asked somebody to do something for me, that person would come back and ask for a favor in return. Quid pro quo, right?

Wrong! Nine times out of ten, whatever I requested was nowhere near as significant as what was wanted in return. Say I asked for two tickets to a play; the favor in return would be something like my speaking to that person's group in Newark, where I'd be expected to fly myself back and forth; put myself in a hotel; pay for transportation and meals; and deliver a free speech—about $35,000 worth of stuff—for a favor that may have been worth about $150!

The point is that when you reach certain levels of success, the favors are never equal. Jim tried to warn a pesky college intern that he could avoid a whole lot of headaches if he didn't run around asking folks for favors. I get it now.

Ask any member of my staff, who will attest that if I'm interested in going anywhere or doing anything that costs money, the first thing that staffer says is: "Mr. Smiley would like to inquire about purchasing tickets."

Now, as it was for Big Jim, some people insist on gifting me tickets. If that's the case . . . well, I reserve the right to graciously accept. However, I still insist they charge me for something, perhaps two of the four tickets. Basically, I try to never ask for freebies. Consequently, I don't spend my life returning unequal favors.

We all know people who, whenever their names pop up on the Caller ID, provoke an automatic response: "Oh, no, no, no. They want something!"

Believe me, you want to avoid landing on that "Oh, Lord, he/she wants something" list. Not only is it a lonely place, it's also no way to build a career, advance a project, or move you to that treasured and respected place of self-sufficiency that we should all strive to achieve.

## A Hand-up, Not a Handout

Don't get me wrong; no one makes it on his or her own. Jim never hesitated to help me get on my feet. He just had to check me when I attempted to become dependent on his kindness. *Everybody* needs *somebody*, and every *somebody* should help *someone* who's less fortunate and less connected. I'm not criticizing those who need temporary help. I'm talking about capable folk who depend on and expect permanent help.

It's not just young people or the Hollywood and entertainment types either. We live in a culture where everybody wants the hookup, the easy way in. Even before the onset of our nation's economic meltdown, millions of Americans had no clue how to survive without the government's largesse. Some will endure mortifying trips to the welfare or unemployment office for years just to avoid the do-for-self mandate.

Ironically, many Republicans, who staunchly oppose economic relief for bonafide needy families, willingly slather taxpayer dollars on "needy" billionaires and bankers. When the auto and financial industries were teetering on the edge of collapse, they turned to taxpayers for handouts. The $700 billion in TARP (Troubled Asset Relief Program) funds—which helped rescue dozens of corporate giants in exchange for huge regulatory restrictions (arguably not huge enough)—stifled autonomy and diluted ownership. Only a few executives had the fortitude to turn down government money and fend for themselves.

This kind of selfishness and cowardice is, of course, quite different from individuals who, through no fault of their own, find themselves in dire straits—economically and politically disenfranchised. Why is government intervention unquestioned at the top of the economic ladder but roundly and frequently condemned at the bottom? Hookups for the rich with well-placed lobbyists and beat-downs for the disenfranchised voiceless poor, that's why.

## Balancing the Scales

There's a new consciousness circulating among individuals and industries dedicated to ending or reducing worldwide poverty and hunger. It's called *empowerment.* In brief, ideas, strategies, and programs are being introduced that help the poor help themselves with dignity.

It was an amazing tale of charitable empowerment that motivated musician, songwriter, and philanthropist Alicia Keys to aid an orphanage in South Africa.

The documentary film, *We Are Together: The Children of Agape*, tells the story of 12-year-old Slindile Moya and the children of Agape Orphanage, an agency in South Africa for children who have lost their parents to the HIV pandemic. Moya is a member of the Agape Children's Choir. The film captures the children's effort to produce a CD that they hoped would raise funds to build a new orphanage and buy better clothing and deliver other essentials.

In the midst of rehearsing for a major concert and recording the CD in the summer of 2005, the orphanage caught fire and burned to the ground. Yet the children pressed on with producing their CD and clinging to the hope that someone, somewhere would hear their music and come to their rescue.

Someone did.

Keys, co-founder of Keep a Child Alive—an organization that provides life-saving anti-retroviral medications, care, education, and food to HIV-positive youth in South Africa, Kenya, Rwanda, Uganda, and India—learned about the Agape Children's Choir's plight. She invited the children to perform in a fundraising concert in New York where she and Paul Simon were the headliners. Not only did the children raise enough money from the concert and CD sales to build a new orphanage; Keys's foundation works to make sure the choir and the orphanage receive continuous support from all over the world.

This group of children was not seeking handouts for themselves; they were trying to help others whose parents had died from the plague of HIV. Because they felt empowered to do for others, they were rewarded with international recognition and much-needed assistance.

New programs that actually allow people to learn to help themselves and sustain their own lives and communities may be the 21st-century models that provide a genuine alternative to government dependency. Programs and projects like the Agape Children's Choir aren't seeking undeserved or unwarranted favors or handouts, just a hand-up to dignity and self-sufficiency. We're talking about dependence versus independence, respect versus disrespect. When you respect and support human beings' innate desire to do for self, you oftentimes find that people, including the indigent, are more than ready to operate in their own self-interest.

You don't have to be impoverished to have an indigent attitude. Our relationships and friendships should be of value to us; why risk them by asking for favors all the time? Of course, setting boundaries in relationships can clearly save you a lot of grief down the road. But why lose a good friend because you stepped into the begs-too-much territory? A safeguard is to make sure you always give before you get. Be it in your personal or business life, *reciprocity* is sweeter when the exchange of services, favors, or goods is mutual.

Big Jim illustrated that there's a never-ending price to pay when you ask, plead, or expect special privileges and undeserved access. The hookup comes with follow-up requests that oftentimes outweigh the initial favor. You should always seek independence and autonomy, do for self, and insist on paying your own way—if you can.

And if you can't, perhaps you should do without—until you can.

## TAVIS'S TAKEAWAY:

Never exploit or take the
generosity and kindness of
others for granted.
No one ever owes
you anything.

© Courtesy of the Travis Smiley Collection

# CHAPTER 4

# YOU'RE ALWAYS ON

Everything was copacetic. We had about 15 minutes before *BET Tonight with Tavis Smiley* went on the air live from Washington, DC. The lights, monitors, and microphones were cued, and my questions were at the ready. I was told my guest—director, writer, and actor Robert Townsend—had arrived at the California studio. The plan was to discuss his new film, *B.A.P.S (Black American Princesses)*, starring Halle Berry. I was looking forward to an engaging conversation about the new film and other matters.

"Yo, Tavis, you seen the movie; how was it?" a crew member asked.

Now, I love Townsend's work. *Hollywood Shuffle, The Five Heartbeats*—great movies. *B.A.P.S*, on the other hand: hated it!

"Man, the movie was so horrible. It was the worst piece of sh** I have ever seen in my life," I told my crew, adding, "and what I really can't understand is why Halle would allow herself to be in such a horrible movie. I mean it was just that bad."

After a few chuckles, we went about the business of preparing for a good show. Five minutes to live air: My director walks on the set. I can tell something is wrong. This close to live air, my director should be in the control room, not on the set. Sure enough, he comes over and whispers in my ear.

"Tavis, uh, we have a problem. The audio guy had your microphone open when you were talking. Robert's in the chair in LA. He heard everything you said about his film."

Oh, Lord!

Now, with only a couple of minutes before show time, I opened my mike to greet my guest.

"Hey, Robert, good evening."

"Yeah, so you think my movie is a piece of sh**, huh?" Townsend growled.

Before I could respond, he unleashed a diatribe of profanity. I let him go for a few minutes. I owed him that. It wasn't his fault he heard me trash his film. This was our fault, not his—the volume should have been turned down. Way down.

With one minute left before air time, I abruptly interrupted Townsend's rant:

"Robert, I'm really sorry you were subjected to hearing what I thought of your film. However, what you heard was exactly what I thought of the movie. Again, I'm sorry, but I didn't like the film."

Silence on the other end; I barreled on:

"Here's the bottom line: What you heard was me just talking to my boys. It would never come up on the air. I am a professional and you are a professional. We are going to go on the air, and for the next hour we're going to be professionals."

More silence. Thirty seconds to go. Negotiation was out the window.

"OK, I hear your silence and it is profound," I continued. "Let me just promise you, I will be a professional as long as you're a professional." I didn't want to sound threatening, but with just a few seconds to go, I had to let him know that I wasn't interested in an on-air feud. "If you try to clown me for what happened off the air, I'm going there with you," I said. "If you act a fool, I'll be a bigger fool. We can deal with this later, but not on the air. Again, I apologize. Let's go."

More silence. The tension hung like a soaking-wet quilt on a thin clothesline.

Now, we're on air live. I introduce my guest, highlighting his movie-making career and mentioning that he's about to release a movie starring Halle Berry.

"So, Robert, how you doing tonight?"

"Fine."

"Thanks for coming on."

"Uh-huh."

"This is your fifth film now, right?"

"Yeah."

"What was it like working with Halle Berry?"

"Great."

I could not believe what was happening. This brother planned to sit there on the air and stoically utter one-word, monosyllabic answers. There was no way we could sustain a one-hour conversation like this.

The show was live, but we took phone calls every night. Quicker than I ever had with previous guests, I told the audience that we were going to take a commercial break, and afterward I said: "Let's take as many calls as possible for my guest, Robert Townsend."

Thankfully, the first caller showered Townsend with love. He listed movies Townsend had made that he thoroughly enjoyed and complimented him as a pioneer in Black film.

Townsend might have been furious with me, but he wasn't going to be rude to his fans. Getting myself out of the way and letting callers drive the show were key factors in flipping a volatile script and turning lemons into lemonade. The show went reasonably well; afterward, he dressed me down again. He called BET's founder, Bob Johnson, to complain. Without the clock ticking away toward airtime, I was better able to address the situation. I wrote Townsend a letter. Even though my engineer's gaffe allowed Townsend to hear me dismiss his movie, I was responsible for speaking negatively about a guest before inviting him into my figurative house. It was a mistake.

I have seen Townsend since the interview; he's cordial when we meet. I can only hope and believe my letter and sincere apology were accepted.

# Watch Your Mouth

I'm not the first and won't be the last to pay the price for a "live" microphone mistake.

Live mikes caught President Obama calling Kanye West a "jackass" and Vice President Joe Biden dropping the F-bomb when health-care legislation was passed. A few years back, during a break before appearing on a FOX News program, the Rev. Jesse Jackson made a huge faux pas when the microphone pinned to his lapel picked up his frustrated comments about wanting to castrate Obama. George W. Bush, standing before a cluster of microphones while campaigning for president, was overheard calling a *New York Times* reporter a "major league a——hole." Evangelist Pat Robertson had egg smeared all over his face during a CNN interview when his description of a departing guest as a "homo" went out over the air.

At least my unintentional movie critique didn't have the potential of setting off a major world war as did the words of former President Ronald Reagan:

"My fellow Americans, I am pleased to tell you I just signed legislation which outlaws Russia forever. The bombing begins in five minutes," the "Great Communicator" joked during a pre-speech mike check that actually went live.

The microphone mishaps of notables (mine included) begin to pale in comparison to today's social-media-dominated society. Today, there is no "off the record." The mike is always on. Somebody's always watching, listening, and recording. Unintentional or careless remarks can seriously compromise or derail your future. Increasingly, today's breaking news stories involve somebody's digital camcorder or cell-phone camera.

Ken Strutin, director of legal information services at the New York State Defenders Association, writes: "Embarrassing Facebook photos and regrettable MySpace statements are starting to become commonplace in presentencing reports and disposition hearings."

Although Strutin argues that social media can also help defense attorneys win cases, the opposite effect, I maintain, applies more often.

Consider the 2007 case of student Matthew Pacelli, a 16-year-old who was arrested after posting a YouTube video of himself asking people to murder his math teacher at his Staten Island, New York, school. To add more stupid to stupid, the high school student even gave out his teacher's name and home address.

If not for video captured by mobile phones, it's doubtful that Johannes Mehserle, a white Bay Area Rapid Transit (BART) police officer, would have been convicted of manslaughter. Bystander cell-phone videos of the fatal shooting of Oscar J. Grant III, an unarmed Black man lying face down on a train platform, were used to convict Mehserle.

Going to jail is an extreme outcome. The loss of dignity, friendships, jobs, and careers are the more common results.

While writing this chapter, I read a CBS MoneyWatch.com article emphasizing the toxic mix of social media and resulting job loss. One example cited was that of a South Carolina cop who lost his job after photos landed on Facebook of "heavily-tattooed, bikini-clad women . . . slithering across the hood" of his police car. Another example: Kevin Colvin, an intern at Anglo Irish Bank's North American arm, skipped work, telling his boss he had to take care of a family emergency. Unfortunately, Colvin's boss happened to catch Facebook photos of his soon-to-be *ex*-employee at a Halloween Party—drunk and dressed in a Tinker Bell outfit. Colvin's story was reported on Gawker.com and referred to as the "Colvin Caution."

## The Social Media Minefield

As the CBS MoneyWatch.com report warned, "Social media can be a minefield for the serious professional." However, it's not just the fact that technology makes it easy to catch us doing stupid or inappropriate things. These days, so many people—adults and children with no clue how it will eternally haunt their lives or professional careers—are willingly engaging in activities that may very likely go viral.

Let's start with the adults.

Captain Owen Honors, the commanding officer of the aircraft carrier Enterprise, was permanently relieved of his duties in January 2009 for "movie night" infractions. Honors produced and starred in lewd and objectionable videos he shared with more than 5,000 crew members and pilots aboard the Enterprise. The videos became public after the *Virginian-Pilot* newspaper in Norfolk posted excerpts on its Website.

According to news reports, the videos included evocative scenes of simulated masturbation, mock rectal exams, antigay slurs and demeaning satire and simulated bestiality.

"His profound lack of good judgment and professionalism while previously serving as executive officer on the Enterprise calls into question his character and completely undermines his credibility to continue to serve effectively in command," Admiral John Harvey, head of the Navy's Fleet Forces Command, told reporters.

Lack of "good judgment" aside, Honor's videos undoubtedly received additional attention because of Congress' recent repeal of the "Don't Ask, Don't Tell" policy, which had required troops to hide their sexual orientation or risk expulsion from military service.

Honors probably had no clue his cinematic contributions would go viral. But because of carelessness, the captain of a nuclear-powered carrier who, according to his commanders, performed "without incident," has been reassigned to administrative duties.

It's important to note that Honors and the senior officers who knew of the videos and attended movie night with other crew members weren't pie-eyed kids. They were all adults acting irresponsibly.

"This is the sort of thing you'd expect from a 19-year-old recruit, but you're dealing here with a 49-year-old senior officer," another Navy spokesman told reporters.

Now, onto the *real* children.

Back in the day, it was wrong but certainly not uncommon for young folks to go to parties, drink alcohol, abuse drugs, and engage in sexual activity. These days, the young folks are younger, the drinking and drugging are heavier, and the sex is even more casual. According to a 2005 study by the Centers for Disease Control and Prevention, more than half of all teens 15 to 19 years old have engaged in oral sex.

Canadian filmmaker Sharlene Azam spent four years researching the clandestine and highly sexual lives of today's teens for her documentary, *Oral Sex Is the New Goodnight Kiss*. In an interview with ABC's *Good Morning America*, Azam said: "Oral sex is as common as kissing for teens and that casual prostitution—being paid at parties to strip, give sexual favors, or have sex—is far more commonplace than once believed."

I guess I can't close this section by telling children to act like adults, since we're all engaging in activities that seem to wind up more and more on the Internet. So all I can say is: If it's not something you can live with anybody—and these days, *everybody*—seeing, think again.

## Turn It Off, For Goodness' Sake

No matter how we shuffle the communications cards, the indisputable fact is that we are all under surveillance. And I'm not just talking about "Big Brother" or sophisticated recording devices in the sky. I'm referring to the immediate and frequently irreversible repercussions of technology in the hands of the average Joe or Jane on the street.

My failure those many years ago to recognize the fine line between public and private speech underscores why all of us— public figures, politicians, preachers, and everyday folk—are required to be more circumspect and exercise far more discernment in the Information Age. If we dare to ignore the personal and professional repercussions involved when unintentional or careless remarks go public, we set ourselves up for far more than Facebook boomerangs. Just ask the diplomatic professionals who have been outed in the WikiLeaks revelations. These unintended disclosures underscore the invisible line that exists between public and private speech.

I'm sure former Detroit Mayor Kwame Kilpatrick had no idea that the 14,000 text messages exchanged between him and his chief of staff, Christine Beatty, would end his career. Not only did the text messages out his affair with Beatty, they also served as the foundation for a lawsuit that resulted in an $8.4 million settlement by the City of Detroit. In December 2010, federal prosecutors issued even more charges against Kilpatrick. If convicted of the new charges, which include extortion, bribery, racketeering, and filing false tax returns, Kilpatrick could spend decades in jail.

In today's rapid-fire communications arenas, we not only have got to find ways to turn the volume way down; sometimes it must simply be turned off if we are to avoid having our lives or careers destroyed by a private moment made public or a public moment gone viral through broadcast or posting over a social media site.

Be aware. Be very, very aware. Even if *TMZ* doesn't follow you around! Be ever vigilant about what you do and what you say in the presence of friends, family, colleagues, or unknowns armed with seemingly harmless recording devices. What you may consider personal opinions or private actions can become public indictments that haunt you forever.

My ordeal with Townsend came before the social media revolution. But it helped me realize the importance of the Three D's—Discernment, Discrimination, and "Do Unto Others . . . "

Social media as a permanent tracker of your deeds and misdeeds can make the stepping-stones to success that much more slippery. Be it public or private, at home or at play; for your own sake, remember: You're *always* on.

## TAVIS'S TAKEAWAY:

Even when you think
you're "off"—you're "on."
In the Internet Age, what's
"private" can instantly
become "public."

© Courtesy of the Tavis Smiley Collection

# CHAPTER 5

# ARRESTED DEVELOPMENT

**M**y freshman year at Indiana University marked my foray into the *grown-up world*. After arriving at the Bloomington campus in the fall of 1982, without my parents' help or permission and no more than $50 in my pocket, it was clear that I had to fend for myself. By the grace of God and the intervention of a few benevolent souls, I managed to get enrolled, find financial aid at the last minute, get assigned to a dorm, and secure a work-study job.

For the first time in my young life, I was in charge of my life. I decided my schedule, my activities, and my food choices, which consisted of lots and lots of pizza. In fact, it was my reliance on the iconic food of Italy and a stupid mistake with my money that really jettisoned me into the grown-up world. Unfortunately, it was an unnerving part of that world that I was ill prepared to enter.

Fortunately, the experience anchored my resolve to never, ever let it happen again. It also opened my eyes to the harsh realities of financial ignorance and helped mold an outreach mission that I still passionately advance in some form or fashion to this very day.

## Candy to a Baby

It's no secret that financial institutions target college students. These days (oftentimes with the educational institutions providing access), banks throw credit cards at students with clean credit histories. And, as we know, inexperienced, struggling students often get into long-term financial debt because of access to these cards.

According to a 2009 national study conducted by Sallie Mae, the nation's leading saving-and-paying-for-college research company, nearly one-third (30 percent) of college students put their tuition on credit cards; 92 percent of undergraduate students use their cards to charge textbooks, school supplies, and other "direct expenses." The higher the grade level, the more heavily students depend on credit cards. The average freshman carries a median debt of $939—nearly triple the $373 documented by Sallie Mae in 2004. Many college students, the study concluded, use credit cards and pay obscene interest rates, not just for convenience, but also "to live beyond their means." So it's not bad enough that students today graduate with massive debt for their education; they also graduate with massive credit card debt and are unable to find a job to boot.

It wasn't the credit card trap that ensnared this wide-eyed transplant to Bloomington; I was hooked by a checking account offered to newly arriving students by a local Bloomington bank.

I was much too young and ill prepared for such a serious responsibility. I came from a poor family and, like so many others from my background, my parents never talked about money matters beyond basic survival. I knew absolutely nothing about handling money responsibly, and the issuing bank wasn't exactly offering training sessions on balancing checkbooks or using credit cards properly.

My checking account became my credit card. It sounds really sophomoric now, but if I needed something and didn't have the money, I'd write a check. Sure, I'd deposit money into my account on a regular basis, but I knew if I fell short, I'd simply have to pay $15 for any bounced checks.

Don't get me wrong. I didn't write checks for clothes, fancy shoes, music, or even textbooks. My extravagance was pizza—one local pizzeria, in fact: a place called Pizza King. I can still see myself writing those $7.14 checks for a large savory sausage and pepperoni pizza.

My naïve rationale went something like this: "The bank will cover me. Sure, I may not have $15 to waste tomorrow, but I'm hungry today." It reminds me of Wimpy in the *Popeye* cartoon series: "I will gladly pay you Tuesday for a hamburger today!"

If I had paid more attention to the bank's notices informing me that I was seriously in arrears, perhaps I could have avoided the embarrassing outcome.

## Check-Kiter

My suspicions should have gone on high alert when I came home from school one day and my roommate, Chi, told me that "Mark, an old high school friend of mine," had stopped by our off-campus apartment for a visit.

"Mark?" Neither the name nor the description—tall, white, heavyset with glasses—jogged any memories.

Not to worry, Chi assured me. Mark asked him what time I'd be home and said he'd drop back by around the time Chi had indicated.

A half hour or so after I got home, there was a knock at the door. I was greeted by a stranger who asked with a smile and friendly tone: "Tavis . . . Tavis Smiley?"

"Yeah, that's me," I answer, still not recognizing my supposed high school friend.

BAM! Handcuffs are out; demeanor has changed; and a new, unfriendly voice barks:

"You're under arrest. You have the right to remain silent . . . yada, yada, yada."

"Un- un- under arrest," I stammered, "for what?"

"Check-kiting."

"Kiting? I haven't flown any kites. What's check-kiting?"

"Writing bad checks," the mysterious Mark responds.

I was totally baffled. It never crossed my mind that I could be arrested for writing checks. I was paying my little $15 fees: I thought I had the process down pat.

Turns out, at the time, the local sheriff's department had launched a *check-kiting sting*. A whole lot of folks in Bloomington, including students, were arrested that day.

Of course, I didn't know all that. As I was trotted out in front of my neighbors, I felt like Quasimodo, the deformed bell-ringer of Notre Dame.

Instantly, I panicked: "Chi, you gotta get me out of jail!" I shouted. Once I was tucked into the backseat of the patrol car, I started asphyxiating, struggling so hard to breathe that the police officer pitied me: "Calm down," he said, "it's not that serious."

It was to a kid raised in a strict Pentecostal environment and taught to respect the laws of God and man. It was a very big deal to a college student who had never in his young life had any interaction with the police or jails.

The whole ordeal—driven to the police station in handcuffs, taking mug shots, sweating in the holding cell until Chi arrived with bail money—took about 40 minutes.

Eventually, I paid the fine and was ordered to do so many hours of community service work—cleaning streets, picking up trash, working on a highway road crew—that sort of thing.

Because of the service work, the incident was expunged from my records.

Still, that 40-minute initiation into the price of financial illiteracy changed my life forever.

## Reformation Man

Three very important personal commitments came out of that arresting experience.

First, unless it was associated with a social issue like protesting against apartheid or unfair immigration policies, I swore that I'd never be arrested again for anything illegal, unethical, or immoral. Second, I vowed to never let money or the lack thereof ever get me into trouble again. Lastly, I decided then and there to help my brothers and sisters avoid falling into any money traps that plague so many people of our hue and circumstance.

For starters, I had to learn how to manage my own money, whatever little bit I had. I learned the meaning of the word "budget"—calculating what comes in and what goes out. Back then, even as a college student, I decided not to live beyond my means. And for the rest of my life, that rule dictated. If I couldn't afford it, I didn't have it.

Since I couldn't afford a brand-new car, I drove "buckets" all my life. The only new car I've ever owned was given to me on my 40th birthday, about seven years ago, as a gift from a sponsor. The furniture in my LA apartment, before I bought my house, was hand-me-down stuff from friends. If they wanted to throw it out, I'd take it in—and this was after I started working for BET.

Of course, I never got rich at BET, but the first thing I did when I started receiving those more handsome paychecks was pay off debt—which was considerable at the time. Although I kept my commitment not to live beyond my personal means in college, I had to make an exception for my family. When I worked for Mayor Bradley, my credit had gotten really crazy due to the fact that, between the years 1987 and 1996, I fell seriously behind on my student loan payments, mostly because I had spent thousands on my siblings' college educations.

There were nine brothers and sisters coming behind me after I went to work for the mayor, and most of them wanted to go to college. My parents were going through a divorce at the time, so I became like a surrogate father. I didn't make a whole lot of money, but, as a single guy with no children, I made enough to help out.

I was determined to get my siblings through school. I made a deal with them: As long as they held better than a C-plus average—I refused to pay for *average*—I would make sure all their school bills were paid.

It was important to me that they contributed something to their education. So, every summer I had my brothers, at least four at a time, come out to California and stay in my little one-bedroom apartment. I arranged for each to have a part-time summer job. Every morning, I'd drive them to work, and they'd catch the bus back home at night. They were allowed a little "get-around" money, but the rest I put into a bank account and applied it toward their education. Whatever was left to pay, I handled from my own funds.

I am proud to say that they made it, graduating from institutions like Hampton, Morehouse, and my alma mater, Indiana University. As I robbed Peter to pay Paul, I relied on a single prayer: "Lord, if you just help me get these Negroes through school, the first thing I'll do when I make it is pay off all of my debt."

The prayer was answered and the promise was kept.

My employment with BET meant that my salary went from about $30,000 in 1995 to six figures in 1996, if you include the income generated through other media appearances and lectures.

As nice money started rolling in, I carried on as if I had no money, because I had never gotten into the habit of living beyond my means. *Financial security* meant that I immediately hired myself a good accountant (who just recently retired), and we started retiring my student loans and cleaning up my credit record.

In fact, I'm always cautioning people to stop spending money they don't have, buying things they don't need, to impress folk they don't even like. Over the years, I've learned how to save responsibly, spend wisely, and invest properly.

And you can, too.

# Exploiting My People?

"Did Tavis Smiley Push Bad Loans to Blacks?"

That bvblackspin.com headline and other 24/7 Internet "news" hits, allegations, and innuendo left me feeling like a man bound in chains and beaten with a bag of bricks.

I found myself in guilty-until-proven-innocent mode after lawsuits were filed against Wells Fargo, one of the nation's largest mortgage lenders, alleging that the company targeted and issued fraudulent subprime loans to Black people. Prior to the lawsuit, I was on a cross-country, free, financial literacy tour sponsored by Wells Fargo.

My role with the "Wealth Building" seminars, as I perceived it, was to help folks become homeowners and invest money wisely. I'd start the sessions by firing up the audience, stressing the urgent need for financial literacy, and building personal wealth—which for most Americans begins with buying a house.

After my keynote speech, Wells Fargo representatives were supposed to sit with attendees, offer counseling, and work to get them loans so they could become homeowners.

The story and its connection to me was amplified a thousandfold when Illinois Attorney General Lisa Madigan filed a lawsuit against Wells Fargo. Madigan accused the lenders of pushing risky, higher-interest loans on Blacks who attended the forums. One of the means the financial giant used to target Black people, Madigan told reporters, was the free financial literacy seminars where Tavis Smiley was the draw.

Financial literacy has always been a big part of my outreach efforts because I take the issue and my commitment to everyday people very seriously. Years ago, I became a victim of redlining and predatory banking practices in South Central, Los Angeles. I hated banks, especially those that refused to lend me money for projects in the Black community. Although I owned other properties, had a nice, steady income (I was still working for BET in 2000 when I started searching for a building) and good credit, for the life of me, I couldn't get a bank to lend me money for my new headquarters.

Fine. I sat with my accountant at the time, Errol Collier, and we figured out a way for me to self-finance the project. My friend and long-time business associate, Denise Pines, found a 6,000-square-foot, abandoned, blighted eyesore in the heart of the Black community. I completely renovated the exterior and interior of the building, adding a 16-person conference room and a state-of-the-art radio broadcast studio where I could produce my radio shows.

In the fall of 2001, more than 1,400 people—among them Hollywood stars, professional athletes, and politicians—came out for the grand opening of my newly renovated building. I could not pass up the opportunity to send a message to the lending institutions that had denied my requests for loans:

"It is my hope that our commitment to stay in the community will demonstrate to other folks the value of economic revitalization as well as show banking institutions that continue to engage in financial redlining and predatory lending the absurdity of their insidious practice."

The next day, on the *Tom Joyner Morning Show*, I escalated my criticism, actually calling out the names of offending banks. A good friend of mine joked about the number of white bankers folks saw walking down Crenshaw beating a path to my door. All of a sudden, money was available for building or any other project I might have in mind.

My answer was consistent: "I don't need your help now but you can help other black people in this community. Deal with the redlining and predatory lending in this community and seriously help Black people get home or business loans."

Representatives from Wells Fargo were among the group of anxious-to-lend bankers. But instead of walking away rejected and dejected, they expressed an interest in dealing with the problems I cited.

It seemed that representatives from Wells Fargo and I had mutual interests. They shared the institution's commitment to increase financial literacy in the African American community. We discussed a partnership that focused on building personal wealth and homeownership through educational seminars. It was the assumption that our interests were mutual that led to the Wells Fargo Home Mortgage "Wealth Building" seminars I began hosting in 2005.

Kelvin Boston, author and host of the financial affairs show *Moneywise*, was a co-host with me on the Wells Fargo seminars. In a 2009 interview with the *Washington Independent*, Boston added needed perspective on the roles we actually played in the seminars' orchestration.

"We all thought at the time that we were doing a positive thing," Boston recalls. After so many years of redlining and restricted access to credit, partnering with a major bank interested in outreach to the Black community was considered an encouraging development.

"Were we probably used? We probably were. If I had the chance to do it over again, would I do it in a different manner? Probably."

But the damning allegations against Wells Fargo made it impossible for me to stay affiliated with the company. So in 2009 I dropped Wells Fargo as a partner, even though the company was a major sponsor of my "State of the Black Union" symposia.

However, that didn't stop the Internet-instigated campaign that had thousands of Black folks asking how much I got paid to play a role in the scam or saying things like: "Tavis Smiley is evil!" or "Smiley led Black folk to hell!" or "Tavis had to know about this!"

I suppose it's easier to demonize a personality than an organization. For example, in February 2009, Wells Fargo and the National Urban League co-sponsored *The Foreclosure Workbook: The Complete Guide to Understanding Foreclosure and Saving Your Home*. In March 2009, the NAACP filed lawsuits against Wells Fargo and a number of suspected predatory lenders, alleging racial bias in their subprime lending businesses. By April 2010, the NAACP and

Wells Fargo had reached an agreement that allowed the NAACP to review its lending practices. The NAACP did not seek monetary damages in its suit, but said it sought to change behavior in the mortgage-lending industry. Wells Fargo served as the lead sponsor of the NAACP's 101st annual convention in July 2010.

Starting in 2011, a new alliance with Wells Fargo & Company and the Citizenship Education Fund—an affiliate of the Rev. Jesse L. Jackson, Sr.'s Rainbow PUSH Coalition—is kicking off a new initiative, the "One Thousand Churches Connected Save Our Homes Financial Literacy Program." This is an unprecedented collaboration between a major civil rights organization and an institution accused of targeting Black people for its own gain.

I believe the Urban League, the NAACP, and the Rainbow PUSH Coalition are just as sincere as I am about providing educational resources that may improve the financial success of African Americans. As I said, it's much easier to target an individual than it is an organization.

I remain committed to spreading a message of self-determination through financial literacy to African Americans and to all who will listen. In an attempt to get up and fail up, I devote significant time on my radio and television platforms trying to thoroughly dissect the subprime mess and its exploitation of Black and brown people, which, if we're honest, caught a whole lot of people much savvier than me by surprise. The "Road to Wealth" segments on my PBS show features folks like Maria Bartiromo, host of CNBC's *Closing Bell*;

Ken Wade, CEO of NeighborWorks America; and Katty Kay, BBC correspondent and co-author of *Womenomics: Write Your Own Rules for Success*. The segments are designed to deliver information about building personal wealth, finding affordable housing and suitable loans, and other needed information.

The financially illiterate are most often shut out of the mainstream borrowing or credit processes. They find themselves victims of predatory lenders like payday loan companies, where they borrow money using their next paycheck as collateral. According to the Woodstock Institute, a nonprofit research and policy organization, minority and low-income consumers often end up paying 400 percent to 600 percent in interest and fees on these caustic loans and this last-resort system of credit.

As long as I have a public voice, I will use my platforms to help people get their money right and their financial houses in order. The Wells Fargo fiasco only made me wiser. And more determined. I'm doing the same free financial literacy seminar; this time it's called "The Nationwide On Your Side® Tour with Tavis Smiley," sponsored by Nationwide Insurance. The seminars backed by surveys provide valuable information—financial basics, retirement planning, employment opportunities, and more.

Why? Because fiscal accountability is an individual responsibility, and I believe that information is power. Knowledge is power. But getting that knowledge to the proper source is challenging. There's no excuse these days for being financially illiterate. Comprehensive data about how to prepare for a secure financial future are abundant. But in environments with 50 percent high school dropout rates, where parents have had little experience with proper money management—"comprehensive data" aren't enough.

With the proper weaponry, we can win this battle. When we arm ourselves with good information, we can make better financial choices. When we make better choices, we live better lives. And when we live better lives, we leave greater legacies. And if one of your primary goals is not to ensure that your children and grandchildren have more opportunity than you, then what's it all about?

All I know is that I'm just a former check-kiter trying to help others fly right.

## TAVIS'S TAKEAWAY:

Don't spend what you don't have, to buy what you don't need, to impress folk you don't even like. Spend, save, and invest wisely.

**ROBERT L. JOHNSON**
Chairman & Chief Executive Officer

March 23, 2001

**VIA FACSIMILE &**
**OVERNIGHT DELIVERY**

Mr. Tavis Smiley
c/o Babette Perry
8942 Wilshire Blvd.
Beverly Hills, CA 90211

**Talent Agreement ("Agreement") dated as of March 28, 2000 by and**
**between Tavis Smiley and Black Entertainment Television, Inc.**
**("BET")**

Dear Tavis:

Please be advised that pursuant to Section III (E) of the Agreement, BET hereby terminates the Agreement effective immediately. Accordingly, within seven (7) business days from receipt of this letter, you will be paid the remaining compensation due through the end of the Engagement Period under the Agreement.

Should you have any questions, concerns or comments, please feel free to contact me.

Sincerely,

Robert L. Johnson

BLACK ENTERTAIMENT TELEVISION
ONE BET PLAZA, 1235 W STREET N.E, WASHINGTON, DC 20018-1211
TEL: (202) 608-2442  FAX: (202) 608-2593

© Courtesy of the Tavis Smiley Collection

# CHAPTER 6

# A PINK SLIP CAN FIRE YOU UP!

Lawrence Harvey Zeiger was doing all right for himself: He had hosted local radio and TV shows and by 1971, he had a gig as a weekly columnist for the *Miami Beach Sun* and served as the color commentator for the Miami Dolphins on WIOD radio in Miami.

Not bad for the son of Jewish immigrants and who barely graduated high school. The impoverished Brooklyn, New York, kid had a serendipitous entrée into radio. In 1957, he worked as a janitor at a small Miami radio station. When an announcer suddenly quit one night, the station's manager instantaneously—desperately—decided to put the janitor on the air. After his impromptu but apparently impressive debut, Zeiger was hired as a news and sports commentator at $55 a week.

Today, Lawrence Harvey Zeiger goes by the name of Larry King.

After a steady ascent, King's world crashed in December 1971. A former business partner sued him, and King was arrested and charged with grand larceny. Even before his day in court, he was fired from his radio, television, and newspaper jobs.

King pleaded no contest to passing a bad check; the larceny charge was dropped.

Four years later he was rehired by WIOD to host an evening interview show. By 1978, his career had recovered to the point that he was offered a late-night talk show, *The Larry King Show*. It was a stepping-stone to a 25-year legacy, *Larry King Live*, which premiered on the Cable News Network (CNN) in 1985.

A dream deferred, disgraced, and deep in debt, King must have carried an unimaginable extra burden in the early 1970s when not one but three jobs disappeared at once.

Yet there's a lesson in King's depressing tale. Sometimes in order to fulfill our destinies, either we're pushed or we force ourselves to jump into the unknown. Getting to your designated place in life often boils down to constant motion versus forward motion. The difference is as distinct as my running ten miles on my treadmill inside my house or going outside and running ten miles through the streets of Los Angeles. The first is an example of constant motion; the second, of course, of forward motion. Many of us don't make the distinction. We think just because we're moving in life that we're moving forward.

If you're going to truly advance, sometimes the jump, the push, or the pink slip is a prerequisite.

By the end of 2008, 2.6 million Americans had lost their jobs. The country's recession, which began in 2007, resulted in the highest percentage of annual job loss since the end of World War II. Hundreds of thousands more jobs disappeared in the succeeding two years, with an unemployment rate at a staggering 9.6 percent in September 2010.

What does all this mean? It means a whole lot of people were pushed into the unknown.

King lost three jobs at once. But he didn't stay stagnant once he was cleared of the larceny charge. He wrote articles and took on radio gigs in smaller markets, all the while inching toward his destiny—defining the real Larry King.

His story is one of many that reinforce the need to get yourself in forward motion.

Mine is but another.


## Thank You, Bob

Not a year goes by where one or two of my close friends don't fail to suggest that I send Bob Johnson, founder of Black Entertainment Television (BET), a gift for firing me.

In my memoir, *What I Know For Sure*, I detail some of my beginning and ending with BET. At the time of its writing, what I did not know was the profound impact it would have on my forward motion. I do now.

To recap briefly, I went to work for BET in 1996. When it hired me, I was still doing national weekly commentaries on the *Tom Joyner Morning Show*, which I continued. My contract also allowed me to form my own production company. In that respect, I produced a number of programs on my own; the most familiar was the "State of the Black Union" symposia, which I also hosted every year. Ironically, in all the years I was at BET, conducting those conversations with high-profile Black Americans, BET had no interest in airing them. It already had its poster boy for serious Black dialogue on five nights a week. It was perfectly content with the 99-to-1 entertainment/information ratio on the network. Consequently, C-SPAN was happy to carry the gatherings live each year.

Don't misunderstand me. Because of the dearth of critical and enlightening commentary on BET, my program became an oasis for viewers thirsty for uplifting and challenging information. My status rose exponentially at BET. I became a household name in Black America and the go-to guy when politicians, actors and movie directors, and Black leaders needed to touch base with Black audiences. The position helped me develop a strong and mutually trustworthy relationship with then President Bill Clinton and other folks of national and international renown. I conducted interviews with everyone from Fidel Castro to Pope John Paul II. In fact, it was a rare and coveted interview that motivated Johnson's decision to fire me.

# America's Most Wanted

Sara Jane Olson—formerly known as Kathleen Ann Soliah, a member of the Symbionese Liberation Army (SLA)—had been a fugitive for 23 years. She and several other SLA members were accused of trying to blow up two Los Angeles police cars. Soliah went underground, changed her name, married a doctor, and settled down in the suburbs of St. Paul, Minnesota, where she raised three daughters and became an active and involved community member. After her arrest in 1999 following a routine traffic stop, reporters were clawing each other's backs for an exclusive interview with her. Katie Couric, Diane Sawyer, Barbara Walters, Dan Rather, Peter Jennings, Larry King—everybody was chasing the story.

Now, I'm not so full of myself that I believe Olson surveyed the media requests and picked me because, in her mind, I was the best interviewer. A number of factors played into her decision. First, her trial was scheduled to be held in Los Angeles, in the same courthouse where O.J. Simpson was tried. More than likely, Olson realized, she would probably have a significant number of African Americans on her jury. Second, her attorney, Shawn Chapman Holley, was a friend of mine. Third, and probably most importantly, Olson's daughters—like a whole lot of white kids in the country—watched BET every day. The girls were fans of my show. According to Chapman Holley, they were the ones who told their mom about this guy by the name of Tavis Smiley "who is really, really good. You should consider talking to him."

I really hadn't been following the story, so I was unimpressed when Chapman Holley offered the interview to me. Finally, she asked me: "Do you know who this woman is, Tavis? Everybody and their mama is chasing this story, and she wants to talk to you."

My jaw nearly dropped to the floor after I researched Olson/Soliah. I immediately set plans in motion to produce the interview independently. The story wasn't exactly BET's bailiwick. It wouldn't even cover the "State of the Black Union," so I had no illusion it'd be interested in an interview with a white, former member of the SLA—that just wasn't its thing.

However, since Viacom owned BET and CBS, it made perfect sense to go to CBS. The interview was recorded, edited, and ready to air. I didn't go to ABC, NBC, or CNN; I went to my sister network because it had a serious news division with *48 Hours, CBS Evening News, Face the Nation*, and—of course—*60 Minutes*.

I reached out to CBS executives.

"You know that interview you all are chasing? Well, I already have it."

They were excited, but their answer surprised me: Dan Rather had been chasing the story, they said, and they were confident that he was going to get it.

Obviously, if Dan's interview aired first, there goes the value of my *exclusive*.

They tried stalling me while Dan worked to secure his interview. In the meantime, Chapman Holley called me: "CBS has flown my client and her family out to New York. They've taken the girls shopping and everything," the attorney explained. "I gave you the exclusive, but Dan's coming hard on this thing, and they are about to close this deal."

I felt I had done my due diligence after CBS told me "no" for the third time. My contract allowed me to produce and sell anything I wanted, so I called ABC. Diane Sawyer loved the piece. ABC bought it, and it aired on *Primetime Live*.

The show killed in the ratings, leaving in its wake a brand-new program CBS had been promoting in that time slot for weeks. The next morning, CBS executives reviewed the ratings and realized they had been killed by ABC's *Primetime Live*.

Well . . . let's just say . . . the stuff hit the fan.

## What About Bob?

From what I gathered, Viacom executives had a few words with Bob Johnson who, in turn, cursed me out. My rebuttal? I had a valid contract that allowed me to produce independently. It wasn't my fault Viacom didn't review the fine print of my deal when it bought BET.

There was nothing Viacom could really do about it. But Bob decided to exercise his executive privilege and fire "uncontrollable" me. The official response was that my contract, which was due to expire in September—some six months away—was not going to be renewed.

I had been with BET for five years. My show was the most substantive of any on the network. When word leaked about my upcoming dismissal, all hell broke loose. Bob Johnson and BET were flooded with letters. People not only called Tom Joyner's show to vent, they also called Viacom so much that they shut down the company's switchboard. When then Viacom CEO Mel Karmazin came to a meeting in LA, he found himself confronted by a crowd of angry picketers demanding that he keep me on the air. Indeed, my abiding friend, Dr. Cornel West, helped to organize a small protest directly in front of BET's corporate headquarters.

Bob, sensing how ugly the whole episode had become, decided he wasn't going to wait until September. I received a letter stating that my contract was immediately revoked.

Thankfully, there was a clause in my contract stipulating that if I were ever fired without cause—which contractually they didn't have—I had to be bought out.

I won't divulge the amount, but I will say it enabled me to get into commercial real estate investing and to secure the building that houses The Smiley Group, Inc.

## Move On!

Tom Freston—the entertainment executive who made MTV and Nickelodeon two of the most powerful cable networks in the history of television—was shocked, embarrassed, and angered when Viacom chairman Sumner Redstone abruptly fired him in 2006. The two had worked together for 19 years.

"When I got fired, I had a feeling of loss because Viacom had been a passionate, long-term relationship. But I got my balance back. I guess it's like getting jilted by a girlfriend, a serious girlfriend. You move on," Freston said.

When pushed into the unknown, Freston embraced it. Rejecting numerous offers from his well-connected friends, he wandered the globe, visiting Singapore, Burma, Cambodia, Thailand, Afghanistan, Rwanda, and the eastern Congo, where millions died in genocidal wars. He volunteered to help musician/activist Bono restructure his humanitarian organization, ONE, and his fundraising campaign, Product (RED).

Media mogul Oprah Winfrey campaigned hard to bring Freston onboard as she developed OWN (the Oprah Winfrey Network). When Freston signed on as a consultant to OWN, Winfrey defined him as her "business soul mate." The new venture has rekindled Freston's early passions similar to when he had joined a group of dreamers trying to start the MTV revolution. OWN, he told *Fortune* magazine in 2009, is about "empowerment and life purpose." The new network is "as big an idea now as MTV was then," he said. OWN launched in January 2011 with 13 million people tuning in, according to OWN CEO Christina Norman.

Had Freston not been fired, he might have missed the forward motion signal. When he delivered the undergraduate commencement speech at Emerson College in 2007, he urged the students to reincarnate themselves when necessary and not to worry about setbacks: "You will look back on setbacks and be grateful for the catalyst that came not a moment too soon."

Being booted from BET was my catalyst. Sometimes, you have to get pushed or you may never leave. If I had not been pushed out, who knows how much longer I would have stayed. I was riding so high at BET, I might have settled for that opportunity and missed the chance to apply myself more fully.

My dismissal was undeniably public: Major networks and news magazines covered the story. I was self-conscious and devastated by all the media coverage. At the time, I didn't realize it had played out in the best possible way. It created a kind of firestorm that I never could have sparked had I just resigned.

I always tell people, "Value is not what you think of yourself, it's what others think of you." You can't confirm your value until it's tested in the marketplace. If I were a can of Coca-Cola®, I may think my fizz is the best in the soft drink biz, but if I'm placed on the grocery shelf and nobody ever comes along to purchase me, I have no value. My value is determined by someone coming along, taking a swig, and agreeing to take me home—for a price. That's value. I would have never known my true value if BET hadn't placed me on the grocery shelf.

After I was officially let go, I literally had more than 30 offers within 24 hours—everybody called. Prior to being pushed out, I didn't know they even knew my name, let alone were interested in working with me. And so I was knee deep with my lawyer and my staff sorting through all the radio, TV, and print offers.

In short order, I went from BET to NPR (National Public Radio). Talk about cross-over: I went from the blackest media network in the country to the whitest media outlet with my very own show. With this forum, I was able to talk to everybody—Black folks, white folks—everybody.

This can of Coca-Cola had value indeed.

## A Lesson Before Flying

More important than the unfolding opportunities, the BET debacle solidified my resolve to never, ever be an "employee" again. Up until that point, I had never really thought about being an entrepreneur. After my termination, I vowed that I would never go back on television unless I owned the production rights. Today, I own everything. I often joke that when I awake in the morning and look in the mirror, it's nice to know that all of my shareholders love me. PBS distributes my show, but I own the rights. The same rule applies to both of my radio shows from PRI (Public Radio International).

With the buyout money BET had to pay me, we purchased a headquarters for my holding company, The Smiley Group, Inc. Fortunately, I no longer have to sweat eviction notices. We started our own book publishing company, speaker's bureau, and a music publishing company, among other enterprises. It doesn't make sense to pay royalties to others for the music used on our shows. Now, we can create the music and pay ourselves.

Entrepreneurism isn't for everybody. Ownership is. Whether you become an entrepreneur or not, take ownership, literally and figuratively. Rethink where you want to go, take control of your future, and experiment with the idea that you have the ability to structure your life and draft your destiny. And remember, content is king. In other words, he or she who controls the content controls the cash.

When director Woody Allen fired actress Annabelle Gurwitch, she turned depression and devastation into forward motion. Realizing she was not alone, she went out and interviewed the famous and not-so-famous—everyone from Tim Allen, Sarah Silverman, and Felicity Huffman to GM workers and her rabbi and her gynecologist. Gurwitch's best-selling book, *Fired! Tales of the Canned, Canceled, Downsized, & Dismissed*, challenged readers to consider the possibility that being fired may be a disguised blessing.

As a guest on my television show in April 2010, Maria Bartiromo suggested that we use our moments of uncertainty to make ourselves adaptable to burgeoning opportunities:

"Use this time right now where you're uncertain about your next move to make sure that you are positioning yourself as best as possible to where the jobs and the growth are right now and where they will be in the next ten years," Bartiromo advised. We should also remember Darwin's words, Bartiromo continued: "It's not the fastest person; it's not the smartest person that will eventually win in the end. It's the person that will be adaptable and flexible to change."

Although Larry King, Tom Freston, Annabelle Gurwitch, and I, for that matter, experienced success after receiving our pink slips, happiness is not determined by money alone. In these times of mass displacement, the goal is to rekindle that American spirit of innovation. Embrace your own adventure. Define your own unique brand of success and sense of ownership.

I love the metaphor, "When you get pushed off a cliff, it reminds us that we have but two choices—flop or fly."

My fervent hope is that this chapter serves as the wind to lift your wings.

## TAVIS'S TAKEAWAY:

Embrace the unknown!
Sometimes the jump or the push
is just the universe nudging you
in the direction of
your true destination.

© Courtesy of the Tavis Smiley Collection

# CHAPTER 7

# REMAIN DIGNIFIED EVEN WHEN YOU'RE JUSTIFIED

I t's hard for me to judge James Willie Jones of Sanford, Florida.

Jones's actions might have been justified. His 13-year-old daughter, who suffers from cerebral palsy, was attending a new school, Greenwood Lakes Middle School, and every day for a month had been terrorized by bullies. Police and media reports say the girl was pushed, poked, spat upon, and smacked upside the head and had her ears twisted. The family's lawyer said the abuse eventually drove Jones's daughter to an emotional breakdown and was reason enough to have her placed on suicide watch.

The last straw for the 42-year-old father came when his daughter told him someone on the school bus threw a liquid-filled condom that landed in her hair while the other kids laughed hysterically. The next morning, he stormed on the bus with his daughter in tow.

"Show me which one. Show me which one!" Jones shouted as he thundered down the aisle. The bus video camera captured Jones's rage: "This is my daughter, and I will kill the (expletive) who fought her!" he bellowed.

Police arrested and charged Jones with two misdemeanor counts of disorderly conduct and disturbing a school function.

In an interview with CNN's *American Morning*, Jones explained that he snapped when he heard about his daughter's abuse on the bus:

"She finally opened up and told me what was going on . . . and from there, you know, being a dad just loving my daughter . . . and just loving all my kids, you know . . . [At] that point, my heart broke when I [saw] her standing there . . . [she] wasn't going to get on the bus crying. And a dad is a dad. And I was going to be her protector that day."

The actions of James Willie Jones weren't at all dignified; you simply don't threaten, curse, or harm children. However, considering the natural inclination of any good father to protect his child, his frustration and anger were definitely justified.

## Bringing Out the Ugly

As I recounted Jones's circumstances, my good friend, Dr. Cornel West, couldn't help but smile at me perceptively. After all, he had been with me when I had used his sage words to comfort a diva in distress.

"Even when you're justified, you have to remain dignified."

We were having lunch at an upscale Los Angeles restaurant when we recognized a well-known celebrity who had become the entrée du jour in the blogosphere. It was reported that the entertainer spied her husband at a party, snuggled in a corner boldly giving "fever" to another woman. Allegedly, all hell broke loose, fisticuffs ensued, and the husband required stitches.

The media delight in propagating the foibles of celebrities. We're fed the sensational tidbits but rarely the painfully human backstory or action that instigated the ugly behavior.

The public was horrified in 2007 when news spread that actor Alec Baldwin had called his 11-year-old daughter a "rude, thoughtless little pig." In a phone message, the actor also allegedly threatened to fly to Los Angeles and "straighten you out."

In an emotional mea culpa on ABC's *The View*, Baldwin attempted to go beyond the headlines and explain his outburst. He and his ex-wife, actress Kim Basinger, were going through a nasty custody battle, he said. In earlier reports, Baldwin's lawyer said Basinger had ignored a series of court orders granting Baldwin visiting rights and had contaminated the child to the point where she didn't want to be with her father.

On *The View*, Baldwin said that he had grown frustrated with his daughter's refusal to take his calls: "Obviously, calling your child a pig or anything else is inappropriate. I apologize to my daughter for that," Baldwin admitted. "There's nothing wrong with being frustrated or angry about the situation. But as people often do, I took it out on the wrong person."

Actors, entertainers, and all those elevated to celebrity status are human, too. Often what's exploited and exaggerated in the media is a reflection of pedestrian behavior. What man or woman blatantly scorned hasn't felt the hair-trigger impulse (fortunately most often suppressed) to whop his or her lover upside the head? "Seeing red" isn't merely a quaint metaphor.

The Internet speculations of the star's fall from the stratosphere to the muddy ground must have contained an element of truth because the red-eyed, emotionally spent entertainer sat with a friend who seemed to be comforting her. Dr. West and I felt the need to go over and say something to ease her distress.

She graciously invited us to sit. We all understood that the details of the disgrace had become irrelevant when I interjected, "Even when you're justified, you have to remain dignified."

That one little sentence seemed to contextualize something for her. A spark of resonance flashed in her eyes before she wrapped her arms around me and hugged me tightly.

Glancing over her shoulder, I noted Dr. West's smile of approval. It was as if he remembered how much his short pronouncement had once meant to me.

# Outside, Listening In

As a child growing up in an authoritarian Pentecostal household, I knew that cursing was strictly forbidden. I avoided the use of foul language until my sophomore year at Indiana University. That's when I shared a house with some of Bobby Knight's basketball players, who were just as foul-mouthed as their coach. It seemed they couldn't communicate with one another or me, even in jest, without an expletive as a punctuation mark. To get my point across to them in conversation, I found myself imitating their crude language.

The players got a kick out of me—the religious kid from Kokomo—who could debate with the best of them but managed to mangle curse words. Apparently, my cussin' linguistics were way off, and they taunted me until I learned how to swear like a construction worker.

The habit stayed with me long after I left college. Not only did I have a cussin' problem, I also had a temper problem. I could go from zero to 90 in a New York minute, especially after my career started to take off.

Sheryl Flowers was the propulsion behind my take-off. In 2001 she became my radio producer and the guiding force of my public radio career. When she passed away in 2009, after a courageous two-year battle with breast cancer, a part of my soul went with her.

If you've read about the legendary fights between Don Hewitt, the producer who created *60 Minutes*, and correspondent

Mike Wallace, you might have an idea of my relationship with Sheryl. We spent all our time together and, as producers and talent often do, we went back and forth all the time. She'd quit ten times and I'd fired her 12 times. But, at the end of the day, neither of us ever went anywhere. We created, argued, and loved with equal passion and forgiveness.

It was Sheryl who tried to corral my foul mouth. Over and over again she'd say: "Tavis, you're talented, disciplined, dedicated, loyal, and organized, and you don't mess around with your money. But there's a chink in your armor. The thing that's going to trip you up is all the cursing, screaming, and yelling you do when you get upset."

To no avail, she counseled me about my temper. Sheryl insisted that I had to be more circumspect about my language. One day, she warned, I would curse out the wrong person at the wrong time and wind up paying a heck of a price.

Her prediction came true. But I had no idea that Sheryl Flowers would be that "wrong person."

One morning we were in the NPR studio going at it. There was a technical glitch that should have been edited out of a pretaped segment that I kept hearing on-air. It happened one time too many, and I had had it. We were off-air, the studio doors were closed, and I was at my extreme—cursing, flailing my arms, slapping the wall, and pounding the desk—I mean, it was not my finest moment.

Unbeknownst to either of us, an engineer outside the studio could see us through the glass partitions. From his booth, the technician had the ability to turn on the microphone in our studio and record our heated conversation.

I knew nothing about this until the next day. The engineer turned the recorded argument into CDs and passed them all around NPR. One of those CDs made its way to management. I was called on the carpet for mistreating and cursing out an employee. To my rationalizing mind, my explosion was just another series of steps in the Sheryl and Tavis tango that we'd quickly get over. But to NPR management, it was serious enough to involve lawyers and to add a behavioral clause to my contract.

After the dust settled and I had endured the snickers, jabs, and suspect looks from colleagues who heard the tape, I decided to listen for myself.

I knew I had a foul mouth, but I'd never actually heard myself curse. But that day, sitting in the studio with my headphones on, listening to my voice, I was shocked beyond belief. The person who sounded like me was enraged and erratic.

That was it for me, man. I called Sheryl, apologized deeply, and promised to stop cursing. I couldn't promise that the perfectionism that sometimes fuels my anger and disappointment about all things work-related would disappear, but I assured her that she would never, ever hear me curse again.

"Never?" Sheryl's response reminded me of Chris Rock's joke about Tiger Woods's promise to never stray: "Tiger don't say never; just say you gonna do your best!"

Sheryl simply asked that I do my best.

Listening to my raging, vulgar voice on that CD set me straight.

It's been seven years, and I've kept my promise.

## If We Could Only Hear Ourselves

Regrettably my unexamined behavior seven years ago seems to be part of a growing epidemic of unconscious, unjustified, and uncivil behavior. Today, we all live in an increasingly uncivil society, where everybody feels justified to be undignified. Fired CNN host Rick Sanchez apparently believed that his criticizing all Jews was a reasonable retort to the ribbings he received from one Jewish comedian—Jon Stewart, host of *The Daily Show*. Students (and some of their parents) feel no regret if they curse their teachers. Getting flipped off in traffic is a common occurrence. The anonymous aspect of the Internet gives opinionated cowards license to write the vilest, most demeaning comments when responding online to articles or opinions published in newspapers and magazines. Folks who could never say these things to your face become big bad dogs online. Has the definition of "free speech" been amended to include the right to "demean and hurt" without censure?

During the 2010 annual conference of the American Educational Research Association, attendees were presented with the results of an online survey involving 339 faculty members. The study conducted by three researchers at the University of Redlands (California) focused on faculty members' experiences with incivility at the hands of students. The types of student incivility ranged from sleeping or texting in class to more disruptive behavior—open expressions of anger, impatience, or derision. According to the *Chronicle of Higher Education*, which summarized the study, "When it comes to being rude, disrespectful, or abusive to their professors, students appear most likely to take aim at women, the young, and the inexperienced."

Nearly 70 percent of those questioned in another Associated Press–Ipsos 2005 poll believe that people are ruder than they were 20 or 30 years ago. The interesting finding in the poll was that very few in that number admitted their roles in a rude society. Slightly more than 37 percent of the 1,001 adults polled did admit to using a swear word in public. But only 13 percent said they'd ever made an obscene gesture while driving, and a mere 8 percent claimed to have used cell phones in "loud or annoying" ways around others.

When asked about incivility in our society, people will admit it's prevalent and point accusatory fingers at parents, rap music, movies, terrorism, commercialism, and a bunch of other "isms," but rarely do they acknowledge or accept personal responsibility for their role in society's devolution.

The disrespect virus has also been multiplying exponentially in the political arena—a Congressman shouts "you lie" at the President of the United States during a nationally televised speech; a former Vice President instructs a senator to "Go fu\*\* yourself";

the President speculates about whose "ass to kick" during a *Today* show interview; political advertising drenched in cut-throat, personal attacks, and destructive lies—nobody balances the justified with the dignified anymore.

That old cliché—"It's not whether you win or lose; it's how you play the game"—doesn't apply anymore either. Not only is the maxim destructive in politics, it doesn't apply on the job, on Wall Street, or in our personal relationships. For the most part, we're interested only in the game of scoring points, taking out our enemies in the most take-no-prisoners public fashion. Society's civility-versus-incivility balance beam is tipping toward the latter. We are creating an environment where rude, aggressive, and abusive behavior is socially acceptable. Instead of finding ways to articulate or deal with hurt and anger, we're settling for uncivil redress. And there's a thin line between a rude response and an aggressive one.

Therein is the doorway in which a caring father was transformed into an aggressive brute.

I often find myself wondering if there is a genuine solution to the absence of civility.

The school bus incident with the outraged father went viral on YouTube. Days later, James Willie Jones held a news conference and admitted that he had become a bully. Before offering a public apology for his actions, he explained his revelation:

"If you see the tape," he said, "I feel like I was backed up against the wall as a parent. I just didn't know where else to go."

Did seeing the actual tape online—seeing himself in an infuriated, explosive, and threatening state—did that have the same effect on Jones as it did on me? Did Jones, like me, see an angry stranger who looked and sounded nothing like himself?

## Cultivating the Tools for Success

Just before I turned this manuscript in to my editor, tragedy struck the nation on January 8, 2011. Jared Loughner, 22, attended a political event called "Congress on Your Corner" at a Tucson grocery store. The event was hosted by three-term Arizona Congresswoman Gabrielle Giffords. Loughner allegedly shot Giffords in the head at point-blank range. She survived the shooting, as did 12 others who were wounded. They were luckier than the six attendees Loughner allegedly killed, including nine-year-old Christina Taylor Green, an A student, dancer, gymnast, and swimmer.

At the time of this writing, Loughner's motivations for the attack weren't fully known. We had learned from prosecutors that he specifically targeted Rep. Giffords. We also know that the Arizona Congresswoman's seat was one that former vice presidential candidate Sarah Palin described as a top "target" in the 2010 midterm elections. Palin zeroed in on the lawmaker because she supported President Obama's health-care reform legislation. To emphasize her point, Palin posted an illustration of targeted Democratic seats with a gun's crosshairs positioned over each congressional district, including Giffords'.

Palin immediately pulled the map off her Website after the shooting and lambasted the media for daring to suggest that her images and language influenced Loughner. At the time, there was no concrete evidence linking the gunman's actions to Palin's caustic rhetoric. That fact, however, does not absolve Palin. She and too many other political figures—Democrats and Republicans—have engaged in the type of behavior that feeds the monster of incivility and easily ignites fringe individuals to extreme actions and reactions.

Days after the shooting, President Obama attended a memorial service in Tucson where he delivered a memorable speech about the shooting:

> *"But at a time when our discourse has become*
> *so sharply polarized—at a time when we are far too eager*
> *to lay the blame for all that ails the world at the feet of*
> *those who think differently than we do—*
> *it's important for us to pause for a moment and*
> *make sure that we are talking with each other in*
> *a way that heals, not a way that wounds."*

In a nation where incivility is in our media, our politics, and our everyday life, Obama properly contextualized what we are up against. I wish the President had gotten around to that speech a year earlier, when South Carolina Congressman Joe Wilson stood up on the floor of the House during the President's State of the Union address and shouted: "You lie!" Obama quickly accepted Wilson's apology and—in the process—moved right past a teachable moment. I'm not saying it would have stopped a crazed gunman from killing innocent people, but I am suggesting that we would have been involved in a national conversation about civility long before the tragedy in Arizona.

Years ago, Sheryl Flowers tried to warn me that my foul mouth and aggressive behavior would slip across the boundary of our personal relationship and into our professional and public spheres. My point here is really Sheryl's point long ago: We must be equally cautious about our personal, professional, workplace, and shared spaces as citizens. Intimidating, disruptive, and inappropriate behavior is all uncivil behavior. Incivility feeds society's warlike aggressive notion that "might makes right."

To remain dignified even when you feel justified not to is the shot of humanity that bolsters civility in an increasingly uncivil society. And there is hope.

A 2010 study conducted by the Center for Political Participation at Allegheny College (Pennsylvania) found that Americans overwhelmingly believe civility is important in politics. The majority of those surveyed (95 percent) said civility in politics was important for a healthy democracy. Further, it indicated that the majority of women—nearly six in ten—are more likely than men to be turned off by negative politics.

Daniel Shea, center director, said: "Americans believe in civility . . . and in compromise; they believe in middle-ground solutions."

Shea makes a good point. We all really want to be less vulgar, abrasive, hostile, and aggressive. We just haven't cultivated the social tools required to help us respond in dignified ways when we feel attacked or slighted: Respect. Empathy. Understanding. Sympathy. Decency. Self-discipline. Love.

Success—personal, professional, and societal—mandates that we cultivate and master these tools that help us gain control, self-respect, and respect for others. When we conduct ourselves with dignity, we walk through the world with an inviolable sense of respect that invites emulation. Respect for others means we commit to making sacrifices. We sacrifice the temporary gratification of ego. We restrain the psychological trigger that can turn our words into weapons. We forfeit the emotional rewards derived from acting out, losing control, or reacting violently—even when we feel justified in doing so.

After the humiliating ordeal at NPR, Sheryl didn't beat me down or say, "I tried to warn you." She knew me well enough to know that the CD shocked me out of my vulgarity. "Just do your best," my dear departed friend said after I promised to correct my incorrect behavior.

I'm still working to better my best.

I believe the entertainer mentioned earlier hugged me tightly because she needed validation. She needed someone to say, "I understand." But I think, in losing her cool, she saw a part of herself that caused her great grief and shame. In me, she recognized a fellow traveler on the dark side of incivility.

Believe me, I know the value of having someone close who at least understands why you did what you did. I'm glad I had a dear friend nearby in one of my darkest hours . . . a friend who wisely shared with me: "Even when you're justified, you have to remain dignified."

## TAVIS'S TAKEAWAY:

Success becomes failure when you lose your civility and your dignity.

© Bevil Knapp/TIME & LIFE Images/Getty Images

# CHAPTER 8

# DO YOUR HOMEWORK

**W**e all make honest mistakes. There's no way I've been talking on TV and radio for 20 years without the occasional on-air faux pas. But I'm the kind of guy who prides himself on being prepared for any endeavor. No matter the situation—be it delivering speeches, conducting interviews, or presenting commentaries on my radio and TV programs—I like to avoid scripts, cue cards, and TelePrompters®. I excel in studied spontaneity. And the more homework I do, the better prepared I am to share the fruits of engaged conversation. With a combination of preparation, confidence, genuine interest in my subjects, intellectual curiosity, and occasional doses of wit, good on-air conversation can appear effortless.

In my world, honest mistakes, even for those who prefer scripts, are acceptable. Not doing your homework is not. There is a difference. Making a mistake is embarrassing. Failure to validate or back up your findings can ruin a promising career.

Consider the case of Dan Rather. A year short of his 25th anniversary as anchor of the CBS *Evening News*, and what happens? One apparently flawed report aired on *60 Minutes II* about the special treatment that George W. Bush received as a member of the Texas Air National Guard, and Rather's misstep escalated into a career failure.

CBS had to admit it had been "misled" about the authenticity of the documents that disparaged Bush and launched an independent investigation. With storm clouds brewing, *60 Minutes II* was abruptly canceled; Rather stepped down as the *Evening News* anchor and—on June 20, 2006—left CBS altogether.

A lifelong record of excellence was tarnished because the homework hadn't been done.

Now, there are some media folk who seem to succeed despite sloppy standards. Since "news" has become mostly personality driven, the journalistic bar has been lowered. Talking heads can get by with partisan razzle-dazzle. Some can divert attention from their blunders by positioning themselves as victims of "mainstream media." For example, Tea Party heartthrob Sarah Palin claimed it was the badgering by news anchor Katie Couric that led to her embarrassing, incoherent pre-2008 election interview with *CBS News*.

Rush Limbaugh took no permanent hit after he used an erroneous Wikipedia entry in September 2010 that misrepresented a district court judge in Florida. In his zeal to instill fear in health-care supporters appearing before Judge Roger Vinson, Limbaugh described him as a rugged outdoorsman who killed three bears and had their heads stuffed and mounted above his courtroom entrance. These "facts," according to Limbaugh, would "instill the fear of God into the accused."

Turns out, the story was false. When contacted by *The New York Times*, Judge Vinson responded: "I've never killed a bear and I'm not Davy Crockett." The judge's wife, Ellen, was offended by Limbaugh's assertion: "I don't think you should be able to broadcast something nationally if you can't verify it."

I agree with Mrs. Vinson. If you can't authenticate it, don't say it. Do your homework.

For me, sobering, real-life experience has demanded that this yardstick become much more than a personal motto.

## The Accountability Campaign

Throughout the 12 years I spent delivering commentaries on the *Tom Joyner Morning Show*, Tom and I engaged in a number of on-air advocacy campaigns. One such campaign launched in October 1999 involved CompUSA. At the time, African Americans spent $1.2 billion on computers and related equipment. CompUSA—the nation's largest computer retailer then—wasn't spending any money, really, to market or promote its products to Black consumers.

The company wasn't the only major corporation that practiced "selective economic amnesia" when it came to spending advertising dollars in Black and brown communities. In fact, our advocacy campaign gained national momentum when we discovered that these corporations, including CompUSA, were engaged in something called NUD, or "no urban dictate." Through memos from advertising executives, we learned that corporations were directing ad agencies not to advertise in Black or Hispanic media outlets. In a memo explaining why advertising to Blacks or Hispanics was a bad idea, one executive offered this reasoning: " . . . you want prospects, not suspects."

We received a list from an advertising agency that identified the companies involved with NUD-related marketing. CompUSA was among the top offenders. Tom and I chose it for our advocacy campaign to send a message to all the companies engaged in this practice.

For ten weeks, we kept the pressure on CompUSA. We compiled the amount of money Blacks spent at electronic stores like CompUSA and juxtaposed those figures with what the company spent with Black advertising firms. We concocted a strategy that drew angry calls and letters on a region-by-region basis. So during any part of the ten-week campaign, CompUSA and all its branches were deluged with angry correspondences from Blacks living in the Northern, Southern, Eastern, or Western parts of the country.

Of course, during that time, we also addressed other issues related to economic and social injustice. Tom and I launched a crusade to have bestowed upon Rosa Parks, the mother of the civil rights movement, the Congressional Gold Medal before she died. Every day for one week, we called out the names of the Members of Congress who had not signed the House Resolution authored and introduced by the late Julia Carson (D-Indiana). In the end, Carson had obtained all the signatures she needed. In June of 1999, when President Bill Clinton bestowed Rosa Parks with the medal, Tom and I were seated in the Capitol Rotunda as guests of honor.

## The Smokin' Gun

Meanwhile, the CompUSA campaign proceeded with no retreat or response from the company. To kick things up a notch, we asked our listeners to send us copies of their CompUSA receipts. They flowed in by the hundreds and thousands. In turn, we shipped boxes and boxes to CompUSA to prove that Black folk spent millions with the company.

This peaceful protest still wasn't enough to make it change course.

Then quite unexpectedly, I received a document I felt certain would tip the scales.

We had a few insiders at CompUSA. One of them, I believed, sent us the smoking gun—a fax, on company letterhead, with the name of a CompUSA senior vice president affixed. The missive urged me to break the news that the company had no African Americans on its board of directors. "No Black members of the board," from an authentic source—that was enough for me. I anxiously read the letter on the air, even giving out the name of the executive who sent it.

One problem: It was a complete and utter hoax.

CompUSA called; there was no senior VP at the company with a name matching the one I had given on the air. The media had a field day with my mistake. I had egg all over my face. I have always considered myself a credible social commentator. Simply put, I dropped the ball. The failure to fact check forced me to give CompUSA, the target of our protest, a public apology:

"This is not up to my standards," I apologized on-air. "I did not do my homework and literally did not check all the facts. I got burned. I'm sorry."

## Standoff at High Noon

Emboldened by my mistake, CompUSA decided to solicit the help of the ABC Radio Network—the company that syndicated Tom's show. In the ninth week of our ten-week campaign, Tom and I received a phone call from executives at ABC Radio: "Either you guys pull up off of CompUSA, or we'll pull the plug on the show," we were told.

Tom and I caucused and decided we'd go on the air and play it by ear. The next day, ABC brass were listening. They had already called Tom's engineer and directed him to prepare a *The Best of the Tom Joyner Morning Show* backup tape. If either of us even mentioned CompUSA, they were prepared to immediately pull the plug on the show.

With our livelihoods on the line, Tom urged our audience to stay tuned: "It's Thursday; Tavis is on today. You'll want to hear this commentary. It may be his last."

Rather than check CompUSA that day, I felt that I had to address the radio network. ABC Radio had violated our First Amendment right to free speech as far as I was concerned. If this commentary was in fact going to be my last, I'd at least lose my job standing on the truth. In my mind, there was no other choice.

The show wasn't canceled. No doubt, the decision had something to do with the thousands of calls, e-mails, and faxes that flooded ABC and CompUSA. Enraged Black folks all across the country shut down ABC Radio's phone system that day in New York and CompUSA's phones in Dallas.

The ABC Radio standoff convinced CompUSA's executives that we were committed to the cause. The following week, the company called for a meeting. A few weeks later, it had hired a Black- and Hispanic-owned agency and made a multimillion-dollar commitment to advertise in Black and Hispanic media markets. CompUSA's then Chairman, Jim Halperin, came on my radio program. Although he maintained that his company never engaged in "no urban dictate," Halperin apologized to our audience for not aggressively reaching out more to all customers.

Further, Halperin appealed to other CEOs, asking that they never underestimate the power or the value of minority consumers: "It's a shame this took us off track for a while. I want to sell computers to anyone who walks in the door."

Ironically, just when we were settling our dispute with CompUSA, the company was acquired by a Mexican corporation. Executives at the company, who had dismissed the Hispanic market for years, wound up answering to Hispanic leadership.

Life can be funny that way.

## A Huge Price to Pay

In the end, everything worked out. But that doesn't erase the fact that I put my credibility on the line, and my failure to do my homework could have torpedoed a very powerful advocacy campaign.

That was almost 15 years ago. Today, because the Internet can amplify our slipups exponentially, sloppy mistakes can not only end your career; they can destroy the professional and personal lives of many others as well.

Remember Jayson Blair, *The New York Times* reporter who was disgraced in 2003 after it was discovered he had plagiarized work and made up stories and quotes? Blair, when asked by his editors to produce travel receipts for a story-related trip, quickly resigned with a brief apology for his "lapse in journalistic integrity." But even with his departure, the scandal grew; in-house investigations ensued and reputations were ruined. The Blair scandal led to the resignations of the *Times* Executive Editor, Howell Raines, and its first Black metropolitan editor and managing editor, Gerald Boyd. Although some *Times* officials blamed Blair's ruse on their desire to help an affirmative action candidate succeed, ultimately there was no reasonable excuse for the editors who failed to fact check Blair's plagiarized or fabricated stories—numbering at least three dozen—between 2002 and 2003.

"Rick Bragg, a Pulitzer Prize–winning *New York Times* journalist, also resigned after accusations arose that an article published under his byline and datelined Apalachicola, Florida was based on the experiences of and interviews conducted by a freelancer. Bragg claimed this practice was routine procedure at the newspaper."

There's also no excuse for NAACP and White House officials and dozens of journalists who rushed to judge a dedicated and innocent professional who wound up defamed and forced out of a prestigious government job.

In June 2010, conservative Website publisher Andrew Breitbart posted an excerpt of a speech delivered by Shirley Sherrod, a Black U.S. agriculture official. The heavily edited video gave the impression that Sherrod was a racist. The post became "breaking news" on FOX and other news networks. The NAACP quickly repudiated Sherrod, defining her words as "shameful, intolerable, and racist," even though she was speaking at an official NAACP event.

In less than 24 hours after Breitbart's incendiary post, truth came to light. In the full video, Sherrod actually explains how she came to grips with her own biases and learned to help poor people ("Black, white, and Hispanic") who were denied access.

In fact, the farmer that she allegedly discriminated against came to her immediate defense on national television. The day after Breitbart released his tape, Roger Spooner—the "white farmer" Sherrod supposedly discriminated against—appeared with his wife Eloise on CNN's *Rick's List*. They called those smearing Sherrod "racists" who "don't know what they're talking about." The Spooners said Sherrod did "her level best" to help them save their farm, which she ultimately did.

The urge to use the Internet to skirt hard work is increasingly prevalent on college campuses. To stem the growing trend, dozens of online detectors such as Plagiarism.org and turnitin.com have been created and employed in academic circles. But young people are innovative and technology is accommodating. Just as there are programs designed to detect plagiarism, sophisticated software has been developed to help plagiarize.

The problem in an increasingly technological society is that we can unknowingly create lies and distortions at a tremendous cost. As Rush Limbaugh's case illustrated, it's easier than ever to access information, but it's also easier to broadcast inaccurate information.

The way news travels at light speed these days, anybody can be bamboozled, run amok, or led astray. It happens all the time. If you say the wrong thing and it's discovered, it can reflect badly on you and, with the Internet, that bad reflection can be on display for an eternity.

It's not just media people. If the White House with all its resources and the venerable NAACP can get tripped up, so can the average Joe. Whoever you are and whatever you do, it's important to think about the consequences of slipshod work.

We have to check ourselves before we wreck ourselves. Don't let laziness or irrational exuberance burn you. My situation with CompUSA involved both. But it taught me a critical lesson about doing my homework. There is no substitute for diligence and double checking all the facts. Developing the discrimination necessary to avoid taking everything at face value and promptly acknowledging and correcting mistakes publicly are equally essential skills.

Believe me; I work hard every day to make sure I'm not sidelined by inadequate preparation. In today's media landscape, there's no guarantee that you can bounce back from the backfire of hasty or ill-conceived work. Just ask Dan Rather. "Do your homework" is not just a motto. It's also a lesson for survival.

## TAVIS'S TAKEAWAY:

Double-check it and
back it up or back off.

© Bev) Knapp/TIME & LIFE Images/Getty Images

# CHAPTER 9

# LOOSE LIPS CAN SINK SHIPS

**W**e were very, very young and very much into each other. She was well known in Hollywood circles and I was an up-and-coming assistant to Los Angeles Mayor Tom Bradley. This story is a tad intimate, but the details are necessary.

To put it delicately, in the afterglow of amore, we mused about our past lovers—contrasting their virtues, peccadilloes, and hang-ups. She revealed details about a former lover's sexual proclivities. There was no malicious intent; it was just innocent pillow talk—at least it was supposed to be.

I'm not going to give the man's name. Let's just say he is very bankable in Hollywood. In fact, he's the sort of guy I would love to have interviewed in my later years and gotten to know better.

Unfortunately, as this story will illustrate, that will never happen.

Fast-forward a few months after the bedroom conversation; I was hanging out with a few of my buddies. As testosterone-burdened males often do, we were engaged in braggadocious, bawdy locker-room one-upmanship. Well, in the midst of this unbridled raunchiness, the name of my girlfriend's ex-lover surfaced. Being the absolute Neanderthal that I was then, I chimed in: "Well, I heard this about him and I heard that . . . " and I proceeded to discuss the guy's sexual secrets.

Unbeknownst to me, someone in that group was also a friend of the man I was disparaging. When he repeated the exact details that I had shared—the ex was no dummy. He knew exactly who had spread the information. He called my girlfriend, gave her an earful, and told her that she needed to keep her mouth shut about his business.

Needless to say, my girlfriend went totally off on me. The breach led to our eventual breakup. I cared about her deeply. The tragedy of this story is that my indiscretion severed one promising relationship and prohibited another from ever getting started. What's ironic is that her former lover and I would have gotten along famously, I'm told. In fact we share mutual friends.

To this day, Mister X will not come on my show. He's never expressed a reason why, but I know. Twenty years have passed, and all I can say is that I still feel incredibly small about that unfortunate incident.

I remember being down on myself and telling Big Mama the whole story. Being totally embedded in truth, she said my girlfriend and her former lover had every right to be upset with me. I had no business running my mouth about their business. "Let this be a lesson to you," she said. To accentuate her point, she shared a classic Big Mama witticism:

"Baby, there's 24 hours in the day—12 hours to mind your own business and 12 hours to leave other folks' business alone."

## In Other Folks' Business 24/7

Rumormongering is as old as the art of communication. But in contemporary society, gossip—as a tentacle of the world's most powerful source of communication—has become a blood sport. As an article in *The Christian Science Monitor* a few years ago pointed out, the rumor mill is abuzz with chit-chat about "celebrity slipups and the personal misdeeds of government officials." With the Internet, such chit-chat has increasingly become a gross invasion of privacy for voyeuristic satisfaction and financial compensation. You don't have to be famous or accomplished; just have an affair with someone who is.

The man I badmouthed is a noted personality. Two decades later, I am now considered a personality, subject to rumormongering and blogosphere gossip. Now I'm on the other side where people constantly run their mouths and blog rumors about my personal life, thoughts, and motivations as if they really know me. Today, I really understand how that gentleman must have felt all those years ago.

Don't get me wrong. Every morning I take my "big boy" pill. Yet increasingly, I find myself reflecting on that long-ago incident and how much easier and more damaging it is these days when people run their mouths and dine on other folks' business.

Several celebrities I've interviewed over the years swear that they never read anything about themselves on the Internet. For a long time, I didn't think they were being totally honest on this count. As I became better known, I read everything that was written about me. I now understand. If you take in that garbage on a continuous basis, it becomes toxic. You find yourself getting emotional, angry, and tempted to respond, which—and let's be honest—is exactly what the professional antagonists really want.

This is not to say that some celebrities, by their antics, don't invite speculation and gossip. They do. But people outside the public eye don't really understand that well-known folks are real people, too. It's not easy grappling with the surreal feeling of impotence and vulnerability when constantly caught up in swirls of rumor, innuendo, and gossip without any effective recourse.

Existing in the spotlight means you have to adjust to the glare. It took me awhile to adapt, but I don't pay that much attention to what's said about me online. I'm surrounded by people whose job it is to protect and grow the brand. They are always aware of what's being written or said about me, and they let me know when I should pay attention.

That works just fine for me.

But this chapter isn't really about celebrities or me. It's about something much more dangerous.

## Clear and Present Danger

My experience 20 years ago was added to this book to help me tackle a larger concern, one that has my head and my heart in conflict. In general, I believe that technology is a force for the greater good because it provides unprecedented access to information, education, and entertainment. No one can dispute how much it has leveled the playing field. But, like the atom bomb, stem cell research, or any other scientific advancement, there's that duality of good intention versus out-of-control application. Because so much amplified, unchecked, unfiltered negativity comes through the Internet, many critics identify it as the most powerful and influential mechanism of instability in our society.

Imagine if the rumor I started with a group of guys a generation ago was posted in some sleazy, sensationalized online news story. Imagine if my boys had dispatched my gossip to the blogosphere. Deeply private matters made public. Whoa! It could have driven someone to drastic measures.

That's what happened to 18-year-old Rutgers University student Tyler Clementi. In 2010, two students allegedly spied on him and broadcasted from a Webcam (and later on the iChat network) an intimate encounter of Clementi with another man. When Clementi learned of this public outing, he leapt to his death from a New York bridge.

Much of the sheer hatred aimed at President Obama can be attributed to the rumor that he's a Muslim. A 2010 Pew Research Center poll suggested that one in five Americans believes the rumor is true. "The rumor itself isn't new," Doug Bernard wrote in a VOANews.com article, ". . . but it has been spreading rapidly lately—due in large measure to the Internet."

A few days after an earthquake devastated Haiti, a rumor spread across the entire nation that a massive earthquake was soon to hit Ghana; it caused major panic and sent thousands of Ghanaians running into the streets. The rumor was spread mostly by mobile phones. Jenna Burrell, assistant professor in the School of Information at UC-Berkeley, cites this incident as an example of the Internet's ubiquitous power to stir mass emotion.

Starbucks, the coffee company, still finds itself warding off rumors that it didn't support the war in Iraq or anyone who fought in it. The myth started with an e-mail sent to friends by a Marine sergeant. In his note, he complained that Starbucks denied free coffee to U.S. soldiers in Iraq because they disapproved of the war. The complaint went viral and became fact in the minds of many. Even though the soldier later recanted his claim and sent another e-mail apologizing for his misrepresentation of Starbucks, he couldn't dilute the impact of his original missive.

Today, thanks to the World Wide Web, it's easy to spread false, misleading, and dangerous rumors. And entertainers and politicians aren't the only targets; be you teacher, bus driver, baker, or candlestick maker—doesn't matter, we're all fair game.

Ever heard of spokeo.com? Well, chances are it's heard of you. The new online USA phone book lists personal information aggregated from online and offline sources that can let total strangers know almost everything about you. Type in your name, e-mail address, or phone number, and photos you might have posted on social network sites appear. The Website offers pictures of your house and street, your credit score, income, age, occupation, and other information you may want to keep personal.

That old truism, "nothing spreads like word of mouth," has become obsolete. The Internet is now word of mouth— on steroids. Technology has accelerated the power to inform, misinform, and destroy a zillion times faster than words we let slip between our lips.

## Until It Happens to You

We're all part of the problem. When we read something negative about someone else online and forward it to our list of friends, contacts, and social networks, we're all guilty. We're all voyeurs, contributing to the cultural instability, societal decay, and the Web-speed ugliness that's infecting America.

To some, it's a small price to pay for the reward of global interactivity. For others, it's much ado about nothing; gossip is part of our DNA. Sociologists say gossiping is a way for people to feel important, bond in social circles, stay in-the-know, and clarify positions. According to a 2010 study by the Social Issues Research Center (SIRC), two-thirds of all conversation is gossip. The study's authors also referenced other research that found gossip accounts for 55 percent of men's conversation time and 67 percent of women's.

It's what we do and who we are. I get it.

We live in a brash, totally indiscriminant culture where venting our spleen in public is fodder for a hit reality show or perhaps ten minutes of fame as an agitated guest on *Jerry Springer* or *Maury* or some other knock-down, beat-down, sensationalized, low-brow TV show. You can't even stand in a checkout line without being bombarded by headlines on sleazy tabloids gossiping about extramarital or homosexual affairs, celebrity weight gain or loss, or a vulture-type story of a near-death notable.

As fun as it can be for creative types, YouTube can also be used to anonymously but virally slash someone you don't like or desire to humiliate for chuckles. Why not? Millions are tuned in anyway just waiting for that hilariously funny homemade video that makes a fool out of somebody . . . anybody.

The privacy lane has been unbelievably cluttered with postings of opinions as facts and live feeds from bookstores, hotels, hospitals, businesses, and local girls and guys' "gone wild" parties. We function in a society where it's actually cool to hang folks and businesses upside down on the cross via the Internet.

There is no Internet FCC as a constant monitoring and regulatory authority. An offensive video might have had a million hits by the time you realize you've been slandered online. The immediate consequence of an improper or inaccurate video posting is usually a company or a person's ruined reputation.

Again, I get it. But it's shameful.

## Navigating Through It All

Toward the end of his life, Dr. King delivered an emotional speech in Chicago. At the time, he was the recipient of despicable rumors, public attack, and constant death threats due in part to his staunch opposition to the Vietnam War. In that rare speech, Dr. King—the epitome of forgiveness—really let his feelings out and his emotions show. He talked about the pain he felt from the maltreatment of his peers. The rumors about his communist leanings and the fortune he had supposedly made off the movement had taken their toll. He said he was challenged to find ways to navigate through it all.

Two things strike me about that particular sermon. First, even Dr. King was emotionally disturbed and distressed about the rumors that circulated about him back in the day.

If he got depressed about the rumor mill then, I wonder how he would navigate commonplace demonization and distortions in the age of the Internet. As wonderful as it is, the anonymity of the Internet allows people to express darker, more sinister, and sometimes even deadly sides freely, with no consequences because there's no real oversight attached.

Second, the road to success in the Social Media Age demands higher levels of integrity. Discretion has become so bastardized that you are assumed a liability before you're hired. Many employers now require new hires to sign nondisclosure clauses. Sometimes heavy penalties are exacted for violating these clauses.

A few years ago, *ABC News* profiled celebrity assistants—those charged with chauffeuring duties, setting personal appointments, landscape work, dog appointments, and everything in between. Some worked for the likes of Olympia Dukakis, Matthew McConaughey, Hugh Jackman, Renee Russo, and other stars. According to the report, "Nondisclosure agreements are commonplace among personal assistants, who are expected never to repeat anything they see, hear, or do for their bosses. If they do, punishments range from getting fired to monetary fines."

The point in all of this is that the maxim "Loose lips sink ships" seems sort of disconnected from modern-day society. Ships are safe. People aren't. Loose lips—gossiping, spreading somebody else's business—has a boomerang effect. It can disable the innocent and slash the slinger. Trust is no longer something that's expected; it's something you have to earn. Gossiping in this "no benefit of the doubt" work environment can get you branded early as untrustworthy and mortally wound your career.

Short of avoiding loquacious ex-lovers, in a world with dissipating moral boundaries, you are the best person to control your brand. Make it a brand people trust.

Take it from someone who is paying a karmic price for his foolish deed. I have become a "personality," and there's a big, red gossip target on my back. Be vigilant—for yourself and for your career. Be ever observant—not only for your well-being, but also for future generations destined to inherit a world where boundaries are murky and careless words can be perilous.

## TAVIS'S TAKEAWAY:

There are 24 hours in a day—
12 hours to mind your own business
and 12 to leave other folks'
business alone.

© Danny Turner/Courtesy of the Tavis Smiley Collection

# CHAPTER 10

# GET IN WHERE YOU FIT IN

It's a testament to fortitude when a CEO humbly admits that he isn't best suited to run a multibillion-dollar company. That's exactly what John Sculley, former CEO of Apple Inc., did. The best man for the job, he said during an interview with *BusinessWeek*, was one of the company's original founders—Steve Jobs.

In 1983, Apple's board of directors considered Jobs—then 28—too young to manage the responsibilities of chief executive officer. Sculley, PepsiCo president and the developer of the "Pepsi Challenge," was selected instead. In 1985, Apple board members directed Sculley to "contain" Jobs, which led to the visionary's bitter exodus. Jobs's departure, Sculley said, almost sent the company into its "near-death experience."

Of course, Jobs came back, and by 2000, he was once again Apple's official CEO. It was the perfect fit all along, Sculley said. Way back in the early '80s, he told *BusinessWeek*, Jobs had the "outrageous idea" that computers—which were relegated to the business world at the time—would become consumer products that would "change the world."

Incidentally, Sculley was no slouch. Under his ten-year tenure as CEO, Apple's sales rose from $800 million to $8 billion annually. But a few bad development decisions and intense competition from Microsoft and other high-tech companies hurt Apple. Sculley's forte was marketing. With Jobs, he said, "everything is design." That successful methodology is evident in products released since Jobs's return to Apple Inc.: the iPod, the iPhone, and the iPad among them.

Had Jobs not come back, Apple would have been "absolutely gone," Sculley insisted.

There's universal wisdom in his comments. And it's not necessarily about the billions Jobs has generated for Apple or himself. To me, it's about knowing your role, discovering your niche, developing your talent, and multiplying your rewards.

In short, it's about learning how to get in where you fit in.

## Why Can't I Crack Jokes, Too?

Until I joined the *Tom Joyner Morning Show* in 1996, the program was all about entertainment. For four hours each day,

Tom and his crew entertained their audience by telling jokes and playing music and taking the pulse of Black America in public. Tom and I defined my role as the "empowerment component." He understood that his show could be used for more than just a platform to entertain; we could also empower people; give them information that could improve their lives. So the strategy for my weekly segments was that Tom and the crew would get folks to laugh, and I'd focus on getting them to listen.

I am still stunned by the impact we had for 12 years. The crew did four hours every day, 20 hours a week. I was on for only ten minutes a week—one five-minute commentary on Tuesday and another on Thursday. Yet, the force of those ten minutes became genuinely powerful, especially after I learned how to play my role.

Because Tom and the whole crew were veteran entertainers, I wanted to fit in and thought I needed to crack some jokes, too. I wasn't comfortable with the idea of just sitting back, idly waiting for my five minutes. I wanted to hang with the funny folks. So every now and then, I'd chime in with something I thought was funny. Each time, it turned into a comedic beat-down.

"What, did somebody just say something?" Tom would jokingly ask his co-hosts.

"No, wasn't us; must have been Tavis."

Once I was exposed, the crew would unload the one-liners:

"You think you being funny and cute, but it can turn on you real quick!"

"You ain't in this, Tavis. We done told you; don't get in grown folks' business!"

I'd just fall out laughing. I love stand-up comedy. Sometimes I'd crack a bad joke just so they'd beat up on me. I thought it made for great radio banter.

Well, one day, Tom matter-of-factly informed me that it wasn't so great.

"All jokes aside," he said. "This comedy thing we keep teasing you about . . . I know you like it and think it's great, but this show requires that each person play his or her unique role.

"I am the point guard and you're the forward," Tom continued. "In fact, you're so good, you're a power forward. So, all I'm asking you to do is run the play. If you get open, I'll get you the ball, and you'll score. I'm Magic Johnson and you're James Worthy.

"Let's just run the play."

"Coach" Joyner was absolutely right. I had no comedic timing when I first joined the show. So after Tom schooled me about my role on the team, I committed myself to perfecting my position. I listened for the setup and waited for the openings to score with my commentaries. In the process of listening and watching my teammates do their thing, I developed my own rhythm and timing. I learned how to be the straight man, to gauge tone and tenor, and to weave into a joke without telegraphing the punch line.

In short time, my five-minute segments became a very popular part of Tom's show. I became comfortable in my assigned role, and Tom became more comfortable letting me play that role—which included comedy from time to time. The commentary/comedy combo was a hit. Ratings went through the roof. The show was syndicated to more than 100 markets with about 10 million Black listeners.

Tom knew his team's potential. His advice to learn my role was invaluable. We hit our stride when we perfected the team. The *Morning Show* crew offered balance that Black listeners, at the time, weren't getting on the airwaves elsewhere. Our approach got them addicted to our game. We provided the razzle-dazzle and entertainment they wanted and the serious contemplative challenge they needed. Learning the value of perfecting my game with Tom, made slam dunks seem like a natural part of our repertoire. In reality it was just a team of professionals each doing their own thing to win the proverbial game.

## Use Your Talents Wisely

In today's culture, very few understand the value of perfecting their roles. Everybody wants their 15 minutes of fame; they want to be *the* star. We forget that sometimes the headliner isn't the scene-stealer in a movie. Often, it's a secondary or unknown actor who winds up stealing the picture and claiming the spotlight. The point is, if you strive to be the best in your role—particularly when you're just starting out—you just might become that unexpected rising star.

The key is honing in on your talent and multiplying it with hard work and deeds.

Why is this so important?

I'd like to use my favorite source, the Bible, to answer that question. The Parable of the Talents, found in both St. Matthew and St. Luke, contains variations of a story that emphasizes the importance of recognizing and using gifts to your best ability.

Here's the condensed version (Matthew 25:14–30): Jesus gives three individuals some talents, according to their own ability. One man was given five; the other, two; and the third, one. To paraphrase, Jesus basically said: "Take these talents and get busy!"

Sometime later, the men returned. One by one, they gave accounts of their gifts. The first man said: "Lord, you gave me five talents, and look at all I have done with them." Jesus was so pleased the man had used the gifts given him wisely that he doubled his talents.

The second man showed Jesus that he, too, had developed his talents.

"Thou good and faithful servant," Jesus replied before giving the man more gifts.

The third guy, with one talent, delivered "the poor me" victim's story: "Lord, look, you gave me only one gift. I was so ashamed, I hid it in the earth. I didn't do anything with it."

"Thou wicked and slothful servant," the Lord thundered. He took the man's talent and gave it to the one who had ten—someone who was going to do something with it.

So now, the guy who started with 5 wound up with 11 talents.

The Parable of the Talents, like so many other Scriptures written thousands of years ago, has retro relevance. This particular parable reinforces the popular belief that we all come into this world with talent—a gift, something that we can do better or different than anyone else. But as the story illustrates, if you don't use your gifts, you can lose your gifts.

The parable is written in didactic narrative. Jesus could very well have answered questions with "do this" or "don't do that." No, he told stories. And there was a reason. He wanted his apostles to figure out the meanings and messages of those parables.

That requirement still applies today. If you really pay attention, you glean the message from the Parable of the Talents. For instance, each man went his own separate way; they didn't climb into a minivan and drive off together.

The moral of the story is to find comfort in our differences and to be pioneering. Don't worry about your neighbor's gifts or blessings. Don't envy someone else's gift. Discover your own. Remember, the men were given talents according to their own ability. Since we all don't have the same ability, we have to discover the roles we are destined to play. This may involve trial and error, stumbling before we can stand erect in our individual comfort zones, and even falling flat on our faces.

Learn the value of your assigned role and perfect it.

When speaking to young people, I encourage them to find their own way; discover their very unique roles; and go out and give the world something it needs—something that only they can uniquely deliver.

There's no doubt the Lord found favor with Marguerite Ann Johnson.

As a confused and abused eight-year-old rape victim, Marguerite chose silence based on the belief that "her voice" led to the brutal death of the man who had raped her. It took five years, but a benevolent teacher and family friend used the words of Dickens, Shakespeare, Poe, James Weldon Johnson, Frances Harper, Anne Spencer, Jessie Fauset, and others to help Marguerite find her own unique voice again. She found music and movement through the study of dance and drama. She found a cause to champion as the Northern Coordinator for Dr. King's Southern Christian Leadership Conference (SCLC). She studied African dance with Pearl Primus of Trinidad; modern dance with Martha Graham; and co-created the dance team of Al and Rita, with Alvin Ailey. Before becoming a world-renowned author, she toured Europe as a producer and actress, vowing to learn the languages of every country she called home. In Africa, she wrote and acted in plays and edited the *African Review* before returning to the United States with her good friend, Malcolm X, in 1964 to help start a new civil rights organization called the Organization of African American Unity. The assassinations of her iconic friends—one in 1965, the other in 1968—did not dim her light for peace, equality, and spiritual freedom. The world knows Marguerite now as Maya Angelou, and her body of work is breathtaking. It includes books with titles such as *I Know Why the Caged Bird Sings*, *Just Give Me a Cool Drink of Water 'Fore I Diiie,* and *Gather Together in My Name*. It includes "On the Pulse of Morning," the first inaugural poem commissioned and recited for a president (Bill Clinton) since Robert Frost graced John F. Kennedy with an inaugural recital in 1961. She's been called Oprah's mentor and inspired President Obama to gift her with the Presidential Medal of Freedom in 2010. Maya Angelou, beyond a shadow of doubt, has been a "good and faithful servant" who multiplied her talents to the benefit of millions.

Whenever I use The Parable of the Talents in my speeches, I remind audiences that although the Bible enumerates the gifts—five, two, and one—it never tells us what those gifts are. That says to me that quantity isn't important. Quality is.

That one wasted gift could have been the greatest gift given, but the third man in the story never used it, never put it to work. Who knows? That one gift could have been the cure for cancer or the answer to poverty and hunger.

Just because it's one talent doesn't mean it isn't the greatest talent. It's what you do to magnify your gifts that counts. If you have no comedic timing, don't try to be a comedian. Be you. Hone your unique gift, work your talent, find your sweet spot, and let God do the rest.

What is that unique thing that you can do better than anyone else you know? Young Maya Angelou withheld her true talent for five years, but once she discovered the healing, redemptive, and uplifting power of her words, she utilized and expanded that talent in ways far beyond most.

Perhaps you are meant to be that invaluable team player— the axis of group motivation, persuasion, and implementation. If it feels right, use it.

Maybe, like Dr. King, you are cut from the cloth of servant-leader. Maybe you are destined to lead by serving the needs of the disenfranchised. If you hear that call, answer it.

Be that good and faithful servant. Find your talent. Work and multiply your gifts.

Get in where you fit in, and I guarantee you: When that opportunity comes—and it will come—you'll take that ball to the hoop and score big time!

## TAVIS'S TAKEAWAY:

Stay in your lane,
but own it.

© Courtesy of the Tavis Smiley Collection

# CHAPTER 11

# LIVING FOR THE CITY

*"Living just enough, just enough for the city . . . !"*

— "LIVING FOR THE CITY"
BY STEVIE WONDER

**M**idway through Stevie Wonder's 1973 hit single, the artist weaves commentary into the song that underscores big-city racism and injustice. A young man fresh from "hard-time Mississippi" travels to New York. He steps off the bus and, while savoring the city's "skyscrapers and everything," a stranger hands him a bag and darts off. Sirens swirl; cops swoop; handcuffs are slapped on wrists. The judge cares not that the youth's an unwitting accomplice in the drug trade. The Southern boy is sentenced to ten years in prison.

Swap Wonder's Mississippi protagonist with a wide-eyed dreamer from Kokomo; substitute LA for New York; and replace prison with the reality of hopelessness and the possibility of homelessness, and you have my "Living for the City" interlude.

My tale crescendos with a life-changing intervention that left me with much-needed perspective and an invaluable lesson about the meaning of holding on.

## Boo-Boo the Fool

> " . . . So they loaded up the truck
> and moved to Beverly. Hills, that is.
> Swimmin' pools. Movie stars."

—"BALLAD OF JED CLAMPETT"
BY PAUL HENNING

It was early 1987. After spending Christmas with my family in Indiana, I packed everything I owned—which obviously wasn't much because it all fit into my orange Datsun 280Z two-seater—and hit the road to California.

Mayor Tom Bradley promised me a job after my internship, but he added a caveat: I had to go back to Indiana and finish my studies. I did. And although circumstances (mostly of my own doing) seriously delayed the receipt of my actual diploma, it wasn't going to deter me from accepting the mayor's promise. I had given him a date for my arrival, and, I was determined to show up for work in LA on the designated day.

After driving my overloaded Datsun nonstop from Kokomo to LA, I arrived in town eager to start my new job and new life. To my absolute shock and horror, I learned there was no job. The Reagan era was in full swing; the economy was bad; and California was still hemorrhaging from the recession. Mayor Bradley had just announced a citywide hiring freeze, which applied to all city employees except the police, fire, and sanitation departments.

So there I was, all hyped up, gung-ho, and ready to go to work . . . and there's a hiring freeze. If I had known, I could have—perhaps should have—stayed in Indiana and made sure I had finished school properly. But since I didn't know, I wound up stuck in LA without a degree, without money or a job, feeling like Boo-Boo the Fool.

If not for Eula Collins, Mayor Bradley's secretary, there's no telling what would have happened. Eula became a dear friend during my internship the previous year. If I wasn't at work, I was hanging out at Eula's house. She had two daughters but no son. Eula, my LA mother, seemed to enjoy having me around and doting on me. After arriving in town penniless, broken-spirited, and homeless, I gratefully stayed at Eula's house in South Los Angeles.

A couple of weeks later, Eula found an apartment for me, right across the street from her house. As fate would have it, that apartment is right around the corner from my headquarters in

Leimert Park today. Fortunately, the apartment was already furnished. The owner had to leave town and rented out her one-bedroom apartment complete with sheets, towels, dishes, a television, and a modest amount of furniture.

Now I had a place to stay but no money. Until the hiring freeze lifted, I had to aggressively pursue a "meantime" plan. During my job search, I found myself locked in three uncompromising categories: "overqualified," "under-qualified," and "undependable." Managers at McDonald's and other fast-food restaurants said I was woefully overqualified. Without an actual degree, I was under-qualified for high-tech and other well-paying jobs.

In retrospect, I may have unintentionally sabotaged myself. In interviews with potential employees, I often talked about interning for Mayor Bradley and how I had a job waiting once the freeze was over. Why *would* anyone hire me? Fast-food places have enough turnover, and any savvy employer would hesitate to invest in someone waiting for the freeze to lift.

## You Can Always Come Home

I could not find a gig to save my life. I ended up doing anything and everything I could to make a little money, including signing up when movies and TV shows advertised for extras. I made appearances on *Matlock, Cheers*, and a couple of other TV shows. I even qualified for a Screen Actors Guild (SAG) card, thanks to a quick cameo in the film *Someone to Watch Over Me* with Tom

Berenger and Mimi Rogers. The director wanted a stock boy to ask, "Who's there?" when the killer broke in through a basement window. Out of the hundreds of extras on the set that day, I was chosen. Turns out, my lines were cut from the movie. But, those two words qualified me as a genuine actor. Funny, huh?

The hiring freeze—which lasted more than a year, combined with no consistent income—was getting the best of me. During my internship, I met businessman Harold Patrick, who became a dear friend and supporter. Harold, Eula, a couple of other friends, Mama, and Big Mama—everybody pitched in, sending me a little money to keep me afloat—which made me feel like a horrible failure.

I was barely hanging on, but an eviction notice pushed me over the edge. When my intuitive mother called to ask how things were going, I said, "Mom, I've done everything I can; now I'm being evicted. I can hear Gladys Knight and the Pips warming up. 'LA proved too much for the man, he couldn't make it . . .' It's not going to work."

I was trying to be cute and funny, but holding back the tears was a battle.

"I know you don't want to do this," Mama reassured me, "and I don't want you to feel like a loser or that you failed, but I want you to know that you can always come home."

For some reason, it hadn't occurred to me that I had that option. Accepting my mother's offer, which seemed like the only viable choice, was comforting, but it also meant I had failed. Tears of relief and humiliation flowed equally.

"Mom," I sniffled, "I can't imagine how things can get any worse. I'm going to take you up on your offer. I'll pack my stuff and come home."

That night, my friend Harold pleaded with me to change my mind: "This whole thing could turn around in a week. I really do believe you'll do great things in Los Angeles. I think this is your city, Tavis. Give yourself another week," he urged.

Harold was trying to convince me to be more patient, more tenacious. He had a gut feeling that California was really the best place for my talent. He had no idea that his argument was bouncing up against an eviction notice. The signs were plain as day: *Give it up! Go home!*

"Time's run out, Harold," I said in quiet resignation. It was a Tuesday night; Thursday morning, I planned to head back to Kokomo. Wednesday night, filled with dread, I stepped into the shower. Lathered up, with water pouring from the spigot and my eyes, I experienced my first earthquake. It was a nice little shaker. In that butt-booty-naked moment, slipping and sliding all over the place, I heard a voice:

*As long as you're alive, Tavis, there's hope. It can always get worse. Hold on.*

This may be hard for you to believe, but for me, it was a bona fide revelation. It was a message I not only heard, it was also one I felt, just as real as breathing.

I got out of the shower, surveyed the surroundings—a few dishes broken, furniture in disarray, fallen plaster from the wall—but no major damage. Still, in that moment, when

I thought things couldn't get any worse, things miraculously changed. Like flicking a light switch, my tears subsided, and my spirit completed a 180-degree turn.

Before the earthquake, I thought I had endured enough and suffered enough; that eviction notice was a sign to move on. In reality, the earthquake was a stronger sign to stay put. It took an act of nature to shake up my world and toss me around, but afterward, I was still standing, still breathing, and feeling blessed to be worthy of bonafide heavenly assurance to hang in there.

"I'm not going home, not just yet," I whispered to myself with new resolve. "I'm going to hold on a little bit longer."

In what seemed like a lifetime later, looking at the single can of Spaghetti-O's in my cupboard and my last bit of corn-flakes in a bowl in front of me, the phone rang.

It was Bill Elkins from City Hall:

"Congratulations, Tavis," he said. "The city-government freeze has been lifted. Consider yourself a paid, full-time employee of Mayor Tom Bradley's staff."

# Hold On!

*"I've been waitin' for this moment,*
*all my life, oh Lord"*

— "IN THE AIR TONIGHT"
BY PHIL COLLINS

I am still humbled that—if not for divine intervention—I might have missed my moment. I was just a day away from leaving LA, a day away from learning that my career in politics was about to start, and a day away from missing a life-changing opportunity.

The true meaning of patience and tenacity was, of course, my lesson. I had been given an internship and job opportunity with Mayor Bradley for a reason, and it wasn't to have me stranded and homeless in a strange town. I needed a reminder. Since my friend Harold couldn't penetrate my stubborn resolve, a voice during an earthquake seemed to be the next best thing.

Hold on! However bad things are, *it can always get worse.* Sometimes we lose sight of that significant message. We have to remind ourselves that things can also get better. I was so sure that the eviction notice signaled the end of my time in LA. In reality, it was a preview of the day persistence and tenacity were going to pay off for me.

In our pursuit of success, perhaps we have to redefine the meaning of a real problem versus a divine delay. If there's a solution—even if it's an out-of-reach solution—remember: Problems can be solved. Learning that you have cancer and six months to live—that's a real problem. But in comparison to life's irreversible crises, my problem stacked up more like an inconvenience.

Mark Zupan—the captain of the 2004 U.S. quadriplegic wheelchair rugby team and captain of the 2008 U.S. gold medal-winning quadriplegic team—can tell you about a "real" problem.

Zupan played varsity football and soccer in high school. On October 14, 1993, after a winning soccer game, he and a few teammates decided to visit a local bar. Inebriated, Zupan climbed into the bed of his friend's pickup truck and fell fast asleep. His buddy—who had also been drinking—later drove off in the truck without realizing Zupan was in the back. The driver collided with another vehicle, which sent Zupan flying from the back of the pickup and into a nearby canal. He was able to grab onto a branch and hang on for 14 hours, until a passerby noticed the struggling, half-conscious youth.

As a result of the accident, Zupan became quadriplegic. But because he held on, not only did he survive, he heroically managed to rise above a seemingly insurmountable challenge. He redefined his life and went on to win Olympic medals and inspire millions.

My interview with Zupan in 2008 reminded me of something Mr. Lee Young, the grandfather of my dear friend Wren Brown, used to say whenever we saw each other:

"How ya doing, son?"

"I'm hanging on, Grandpa Lee," I'd answer.

"Naw, naw, naw, son," the elderly man always responded: "Pictures hang; you hold on!"

Hold on! In the bigger landscape, what happened to me in the late 1980s was a small detour. The delay could qualify me as a "failure" only if I used it as an excuse to give up. Short-term failures used as stepping-stones to long-term success allow us to *fail up.* Failing at something doesn't make us failures. Even if things hadn't worked out in California, due to the state's economic situation, that would only say something about me if I let it. I was the same energetic, young man itching to be molded and utilized. Nothing in my DNA had changed. Likewise, whatever happens to you has nothing to do with what's happening inside you. Graduates who can't find employment or people who have been downsized or terminated can consider themselves "failures" only if they fail to hold on to their goals. Recast delays and rejections as practice sessions for the job that suits you.

Ask yourself: Can I identify the solution to my problem?

Am I comfortable with the idea that I may have to chart a course that's unlike the one I imagined?

If you answered "yes," you're not ready for that Midnight Train to what you consider comfortable.

Base your confidence on the fact that you've held a job or graduated from a college that has prepared you for something better, something that will challenge and grow your gifts. Don't insist on dictating the journey. Be patient and prepared and on the lookout for your earthquake moment.

Many times since that ground-rattling incident, I've been reminded that benefits will come if I just hold on to my vision and my commitment to use my gifts to serve. There are no magic wands, but there is the indisputable magic of hanging in there. As noted publisher and author William Feather put it: "Success seems to be largely a matter of hanging on after others have let go."

The people in life who end up "making it" are usually not the most gifted or talented, the most fortunate, or the smartest—they are those who manage to hold on the longest.

Hold on and hang in! As long as we're living and breathing, as long as we have family and friends and people who believe in us and love us—things can always get better. Whenever we're feeling picked on by the universe, striving to accept our discomfort as a stage in our development may save our sanity. There's power in accepting unexpected circumstances and challenges as the perfect pause before completion. Don't give delays or unexpected setbacks more energy than they deserve. Be at peace, knowing that it's inevitable that you are going to get exactly where you're supposed to be.

Sometimes that pause before completion is really an invitation to be creative, to fine-tune your engines. Being overqualified or underqualified may be a signal that you're in need of a tune-up. You may have to go back to school or take some kind of technical course. You may have to volunteer to gain access and skills. Or it may mean becoming an entrepreneur and starting your own business. Whatever it means, commit to creatively charting your own course.

How long do you have to hold on? I can't say; it's situational. I *can* say you must resist the urge to give up. I *can* say that you have to find ways to navigate your way through it.

Hold on! Things can—and will—get better.

## TAVIS'S TAKEAWAY:

Failing is a part of the process.
No failure, no success.

© Courtesy of the Tavis Smiley Collection

# CHAPTER 12

# GIVE THE PEOPLE
# WHAT THEY WANT

When was the last time you had clear beer, rabbit jerky, McLean burgers, or used yogurt shampoo? Chances are, you haven't used any of these lately. Most have been sentenced to the museum of discontinued products or the history of really great ideas that turned out to be really bad ones.

These so-called innovations are all examples of corporations' stretching their brands or operating outside their expertise. No matter how excited the R&D departments were, most consumers rejected Coca-Cola® when it tried to change its formula and they didn't want Choglit, Coca-Cola's chocolate beverage. Consumers equally and emphatically rejected Crystal Clear Pepsi and Coors' clear-colored malt liquor, Zima, as well as its bottled water. McDonalds' and Burger King's low-fat or veggie burgers and Clairol's yogurt shampoo all met similar fates.

Americans expect beer companies to give them brown beer, not clear brew or sparkling water. They want dark Pepsi and classic, regular-tasting Coke. Most fast-food patrons will brave a salad, but they aren't looking for healthy hamburgers. Women by and large don't like the idea of food such as yogurt in their hair. Rabbit jerky may be okay for dogs, but Americans love their bunnies. They had difficulty separating Bugs and the Easter Bunny from jerky.

Stay in your lane. Drive with a purpose. Control your destiny.

To push my driving metaphor to the limit, I Googled "Stay in your lane." Interestingly, the helpful hints offered on the subject by "Nissan Master Tech" have literal as well as figurative value:

"Look ahead to where you want your car to go."

"Don't look at the lines on either side of your car."

I loved this part about clutching the wheel: "Hold it like you are holding your boyfriend's hand . . ."

Taking my eyes off my destination, looking at lines of opportunity outside my expertise, and putting my career in a stranger's hands: These were all part of my embarrassing lane-changing experience.

## The Tavis T-Shirt

What was I thinking? In my career, in my life, I've been very fortunate in knowing who I am and what people expect from me. I'm *not* an opportunist; I avoid opportunists. But a few years ago, when an enthusiastic associate made a marketing pitch, my inner entrepreneur was banking the profits.

"Man, people love you, especially women," the marketer told me. "Let's do a photo shoot, put your face on the front and a couple of your quotes on the back. It'll be huge."

He was pushing the idea of mass-producing Tavis T-shirts. I can still hear my asinine response when I saw the prototype, "Yeah, that can work."

Again, what was I thinking? To my knowledge, there aren't any Paul Harvey, Charlie Rose, or George Will T-shirts. Not only did I fall for the ridiculous idea of putting my face on a T-shirt, I also invested money into producing hundreds of those things.

Long story short: There are a heck of a lot of T-shirts in my garage today.

The moral? Never lose sight of what your audience wants. I'm blessed with fans who expect hard-hitting analysis and insightful or challenging information that is presented with thought-provoking candor and honesty. When I interview people on my shows, they expect me to ask penetrating and poignant questions; during guest appearances on news shows like *Meet the Press*, they want me to raise hidden, underrepresented, or forgotten aspects of key issues. People attend my lectures and purchase my books, and parents send their kids through my foundation for training, because they are confident about the consistency of my message.

If I'm off message or trying to force people to buy or accept something they don't want from me, the results can be . . . well, let's put it this way: Anybody need a Tavis T-shirt?

## The Difference Between "Want" and "Need"

I don't mean to suggest that you shouldn't innovate or experiment. You don't have to be so constrained that you confine yourself to the prison of other people's expectations. Sometimes people don't know what they want until it's presented in a palatable way. In the mid-1980s, people didn't know how essential computers would be to their non-work lives until Steve Jobs and Bill Gates came along and introduced America to the world of personal computers.

What I'm suggesting is that once you've found your sweet spot, once you've defined who you are and know what you stand for, you will know how, what, and when to give to the people.

Let's look at the life of Nobel Prize–winning economist Muhammad Yunus. In 1974, as a university teacher in

Bangladesh, Professor Yunus felt conflicted teaching the "elegant theories of economics" while the country was drenched in crushing hunger and mass poverty. He was consumed with a deep desire to do something to help Bangladesh's poor.

At first, Dr. Yunus used his own money to make small loans to 42 female villagers. The women not only used the money to start or enhance their small enterprises, they also paid the money back in full. Realizing the empowering aspect of this simple endeavor, the economist turned to established banks to expand the practice. Undeterred by bankers who insisted the poor were not creditworthy, he and his supporters created Grameen Bank (village bank) for the poor. In his 2006 Nobel Peace Prize acceptance speech, Dr. Yunus reported that Grameen Bank had written nearly seven million loans to poor people in 73,000 villages. The bank offered reasonable savings, pension funds, and insurance products; it underwrote student loans and housing loans used to construct more than 640,000 houses where women—for the first time—held legal ownership.

Professor Yunus could innovate in his chosen field because he was clear about his role. Because he adopted a mission "to help the poor" rather than tell the people what was good for them, he was able to give the people what they wanted. Keep in mind: He recognized the potential of these people even though they never imagined they could be served in such a magnanimous and life-altering way. In his book, *Creating a World Without Poverty,* he wrote:

"If poverty is to be reduced or eliminated, the next generation must be our focus. We must prepare them to peel off the signs and stigmas of poverty and instill in them a sense of human dignity and hope for the future."

In his latest book, *Building Social Business: The New Kind of Capitalism That Serves Humanity's Most Pressing Needs*, Dr. Yunus offers a recipe for tackling poverty and hopelessness all over the world, including America. "Social businesses," he insists, are businesses that are not designed for profit but are driven by social needs. As an example, he details a joint venture between Grameen and Danone (also known as Dannon), the French dairy conglomerate. The collaboration led to the creation of a small factory in Bangladesh where mostly villagers, given the resources to help themselves, produce and sell fortified yogurt that helps tackle the scourge of malnutrition among Bangladeshi children.

All over the world and in ghettos and barrios across America, hunger, poverty, and unemployment are just a few of our shared plights. There is unimaginable opportunity for visionaries to address these issues, empower the poor, and change our world for the better.

As a child, Majora Carter spent a lot of time daydreaming about how she could change her world for the better—by escaping from the South Bronx ghettos. Education was her ticket—first to Wesley University where she studied cinema and film production, then to grad school at New York University. Money woes brought her back to the Bronx, back to her parents' house, and, amazingly, back to a community she learned to love.

In the South Bronx, she discovered a need and a role for herself that would address that need. Carter told CNN in 2008 that she saw an underserved, ignored, and literally dumped-on neighborhood—her neighborhood in need of support and redirection.

"People wanted things like clean air; they wanted safe places for their kids to play where they wouldn't get hit by a truck. They wanted living-wage jobs that didn't degrade the environment or kill them," Carter pointed out.

In 1997, Carter helped secure a $10,000 government grant for the development and restoration of Hunts Point Riverside Park in the South Bronx. Over a five-year period, in collaboration with other community groups and public agencies, Carter helped leverage more than $3 million to rebuild the park.

That event was just the beginning of a career highlighted by the development of an 11-mile-long South Bronx waterfront, an urban green-collar training program for the formerly incarcerated, urban forestry, green roof installation, community garden projects, and other efforts that are too numerous to list. In 2008, a writer for *The New York Times* dubbed Carter "The Green Power Broker" and "one of the city's best-known advocates for environmental justice."

Carter is a visionary who recognized the people's need. She developed a company, Sustainable South Bronx, and set out to aggressively address similar needs far beyond the Bronx, across the United States, and around the globe.

It all began by discovering her passion and then defining the role she was meant to play.

## When "Need" Meets "Passion" . . . Watch Out!

As an entrepreneur, I encourage people, especially young people, not to go looking for a job. I tell kids to take the word "job" out of their vocabulary: "As gifted, skilled, and talented as you are, I want you to discover your calling, find your purpose, and take action."

Our troubled world needs visionaries. Money is important, I know that. But the sole pursuit of money can lead to an empty life. Find that vocation, that calling, that purpose you are uniquely suited for—become the best at it, and I sincerely believe you will get paid.

Dr. King, quoting Ralph Waldo Emerson, put it this way: "If a man can write a better book, preach a better sermon, or make a better mousetrap than his neighbor, though he build his house in the woods, the world will make a beaten path to his door." My refrain on Dr. King's advice is: Build that mousetrap better than anybody else, and Wal-Mart will find you!

The point is not really about mousetraps or making money. It's about perfecting the gift and addressing the need. When you perfect the gift, the need becomes apparent. If you are passionately driven to serve children and perfect a unique way to serve them, there is a place for you in abandoned communities throughout this country.

We can best give people what they want (and what they need) when we are authentic. If we are true to who we are, our gift will make room for itself. It will expand and open up opportunities for you to do more and to help more people.

In our fast-paced, superficial society, it's hard to get centered. It's difficult for us to get comfortable with our true gifts. Often, as we try to keep up with the pace of the world, we attempt ten million things and never discover our true vocation, our true purpose.

The challenge is to find ways to mute the noise and hone in with laser-like precision on who you truly are.

I believe that we are all here for a reason. We are charged to discover our unique gift and use it to make sure that this earth is in a little better condition on the day we exit than it was on the day we entered. We begin that journey of discovery with simple questions: What burdens your soul? If seeing homeless people causes you to break down and cry, find a way to lift that burden. Let your soul burden point you to your calling—define your passion and audaciously set out to make a difference in people's lives.

When my "need" met my "passion," things seemed to flower and flourish for me. Outside of my ill-advised T-shirt venture, I've learned to cultivate my gifts and think long and hard before I change lanes. Yes, I continue to pursue countless interests—that's how I'm hardwired—I appear on radio and TV, write books, and operate communication and advocacy enterprises. However, none of these activities falls outside of my core gifts. They are all vertically integrated pillars of my passion.

Here's the bottom line: You can't give the people what they want until you know what you really want, and you have to be as passionate about both your vision and its manifestation.

In 2011, I am celebrating 20 years in broadcasting because I had no other choice.

So avoid potholes on the road of life, such as what other people think you should do, or even what might seem like the most prudent thing to do. Be still, get clarity, and always be loyal to what you love.

## TAVIS'S TAKEAWAY:

If you can't passionately
sell it to yourself,
nobody else
is going to buy it.

© 1994, Los Angeles Times. Reprinted with Permission.

**MUSIC**
She may be an opera star, but
Dawn Upshaw's going to have to
take diva lessons. Page 4

**COMMENTARY**
First the play, now the movie:
Camille Paglia sifts through the
truths of "Oleanna." Page 6

**TELEVISION**
Who said the hourlong drama was
dead? How "E.R." found a cure for
the common show. Page 8

# CALENDAR

Los Angel

NOVEMBER 6, 1994

## Talk Radio's Ne(X)t Generation?

They're Tavis Smiley and Ruben Navarrette,
and they're proving that twentysomethings can
do more than just whine about baby boomers.
By Claudia Puig  Page 7

# CHAPTER 13

# THE DIVERSITY IMPERATIVE

**D**r. Martin Luther King, Jr., is the greatest American our nation has ever produced. I've said this many times and stand by that statement. Love was his only weapon. With it, he transformed a nation, transformed the world, and helped transform a poor, Black kid struggling to find his identity in the overwhelmingly white world of Kokomo, Indiana.

Before Dr. King influenced my life, Muhammad Ali helped me to cope. Giving white kids a verbal beat-down, like Ali, was my way of reconciling my race- and class-based insecurities.

When I was about 12, a deacon at my church decided to introduce me to this servant-leader via recorded speeches.

Ali's physical and verbal attributes captivated me, but Dr. King's unwavering commitment to the struggle of Black folk converted me to his cause. I interpreted his words about the Black/white divide in America as a reflection of my Black/white experiences in Indiana. I wanted to be like Dr. King; I wanted to be courageous and change the world. I clung to Ali, but with Dr. King as extra motivation, my beat-downs were now presented with a self-righteous justification.

I was mistaken.

Much later in life, I realized that my view was myopic. Dr. King's passionate words touched my heart, but my soul had yet to fully comprehend the fact that he was inspired by men whose skin color or culture did not match ours.

His influences included the clergyman Walter Rauschenbusch, Rabbi Abraham Joshua Heschel, and Mahatma Gandhi. His beliefs were cemented in the concepts of the Social Gospel, nonviolence, and human rights for the downtrodden. Dr. King came to operate under the umbrella of three basic principles, essentially:

*Justice for all*
*Service to others*
*Love that liberates*

We now live in the most multicultural, multiracial, multiethnic America ever, but evidence abounds that we are retreating from Dr. King's principles. Instead of making progress on the racial front, we're backsliding, becoming less tolerant, further entrenched in paranoid nativism, and more stubbornly embedded in class, race, and political divisions. Never mind that there's a Black man in the White House.

If this country is to truly thrive, it must honor its constitutional tenets of freedom and justice for all—regardless of skin color or class differences. In a globally connected, competitive world, it must shun its narcissistic tendency to stomp on the least of us.

Diversity is more than a hopeful goal; it is an imperative. This was the true message I had to absorb if I really planned to walk in the footsteps of America's King.

## Not Just Black People

In college, as the solo Black member of Indiana University's debate team, my ongoing goal was to dominate through convincing, well-articulated, and passionate presentations. I made sure my arguments floated like a butterfly and stung like a bee; and—just like the famed, Atlanta-born, Baptist minister, I did my best to mesmerize my audiences.

My debate coach—white, conservative, and a solid supporter of Reaganomics—took a personal interest in me. One day, we became engaged in a deep conversation while on a long bus ride back to campus after a tournament. We hit on the hot button topics of politics, religion, and race. Her positions were conservative in nature while mine, of course, reflected Black, progressive liberalism. As our conversation came to an end, my coach offered these words of advice:

"You know, Tavis, it would be a mistake to limit yourself to the struggles of just Black people. It could be your starting point, like your hero Dr. King, but your message has the potential to be far more universal."

Ironically, Mayor Allison, with whom I interned, said something similar to me during a moment of course correction. "You have so much to offer the American people, not just Black people," she affirmed.

The words of both of these white women came through loud and clear, but I had to wrestle with their meanings. Both had proven themselves to be my supporters with my best interests at heart, but in my youth, I wasn't exactly sure how to process what they were saying to me. Was this a dis of my people or a diminishment of my love for them? Had I been cut and just didn't know it? Then again, perhaps I was simply too young and underexposed to the true depth of Dr. King to absorb the full meaning of their message.

My philosophical, social, and cultural evolution came after I left Indiana.

## Race and Power

In his 1993 book, *Politics in Black and White: Race and Power in Los Angeles*, author Raphael Sonenshein defined five-term Mayor Tom Bradley as "the most important political figure in Los Angeles in the last three decades."

Through an internship, and later, as part of Bradley's staff, I was shoulder to shoulder with the icon who put together a coalition of Jewish, Black, Hispanic, and other liberal supporters who beat back racist opposition in 1973. He went on to build a city that was "proudly multicultural," as *LA Times* writer Howard Blume noted.

When I ran for a city council seat in LA, I used Mayor Bradley's model. I didn't run on divisive racial politics, even though I firmly believed my opponent catered to her white constituents while largely ignoring the Black voters in the Crenshaw district. Although I didn't win the race, I came to really appreciate how the mayor's diversified approaches earned lifelong loyalty and empowered an entire city.

After leaving Mayor Bradley's office and slowly gaining access to larger and larger local radio audiences, I had the opportunity to partner with Ruben Navarrette, Jr. He later worked for the *San Diego Union-Tribune* and became one of the most widely syndicated Hispanic columnists in the country. But back in 1994, Ruben and I were just two 20-somethings co-hosting one of the country's first Black/brown radio programs.

Initially, I was hesitant about our partnership. Number one: I was a solo guy; the idea of sharing the microphone with a co-host wasn't immediately appealing. Second: Like my debate coach, Ruben was more conservative in his views. I feared that, politically, our partnership wouldn't work. The only thing we really had in common was our youth, which won us the coveted cover spot on the *LA Times's Calendar* magazine, "Talk Radio's Ne(X)t Generation."

On the air five nights a week, Ruben and I were forced to wrestle with the Black/brown divide. At the time everyone was in an uproar about the vast numbers of Hispanics moving into LA. I was one of those voices speaking for Blacks who felt they were being crowded out by Latinos. Ruben didn't agree with me, but we learned to respectfully deal with our differences and elevate conversations beyond youthful emotion.

The show was short-lived, but in the time we spent together, I came to better appreciate the value of passionate, diverse dialogue; multiracial coalitions; and the importance of stepping outside the exclusive prism of my blackness. We may have held dramatically opposing political views, but when it came to unemployment, poverty, and prisons, Ruben and I were in total agreement—both Black and brown folk were catching hell.

## Start Where You Are . . .

The advice of my debate coach and Mayor Allison took on more meaning as I rose in the public arena and my understanding of Dr. King's principles congealed. The struggles of Black people were Dr. King's starting point, but his message was absolutely universal.

As a twice-weekly commentator on the *Tom Joyner Morning Show* and later as host of my own program on Black Entertainment

Television (BET), my starting point was with Black audiences. But as I evolved, I went from the Blackest of Black media venues, Tom and BET, to the whitest of white media outlets—NPR and PBS.

The same sense of evolution applied to my decision in early 2010 not to host the annual State of the Black Union conference. For ten years, we had rare, high-caliber, and important conversations that were broadcast nationally on C-SPAN. But even before the election of Obama, that void had been filled by a variety of Black media platforms from talk radio shows to Websites to blogs. My role as convener of the symposia wasn't as necessary as it had been in prior years. So many other forums now have the chance to raise the issues that I've always championed and continue to care about. I now have the opportunity to take my passions into different arenas.

The space that so desperately needs the inclusion of voices and concerns like mine is that sphere of analysis dominated by the Sunday morning network news shows and cable networks like CNN, FOX News Channel, and MSNBC. Despite the overpopulation of news and information outlets, there is less and less ideological diversity in the media. So many of us are left out of these conversations. When we turn on cable television, for the most part, all we see, all day and all night, is all white.

In the most multicultural, multiracial, multiethnic America ever, mainstream media is at its best when it challenges folks to reexamine the assumptions they hold and expand their inventory of ideas. Mainstream media is at its worst when it fails to use its power to introduce Americans to one another—when it hesitates to build bridges across wide racial, cultural, ideological, and political gulfs.

This was the impetus behind the forum I hosted just days before the annual celebration of Dr. Martin Luther King, Jr.'s birthday. On January 13, 2011, I had the privilege to moderate "America's Next Chapter," a nationally televised discussion in Washington, DC at George Washington University. The guest panelists were Arianna Huffington, founder of *The Huffington Post*; John S. Chen, chairman of the Committee of 100; CNBC's Maria Bartiromo; David Frum, former speechwriter for President George W. Bush; Dana Milbank, political columnist for *The Washington Post*; David Brody, chief political correspondent for CBN News; Maria Teresa Kumar, executive director/co-founder of Voto Latino; and, of course, my good friend Dr. Cornel West.

For three hours, Americans who tuned into C-SPAN, caught the rebroadcast on my PBS show, or streamed it online were treated to the kind of rich, diverse, racial, ethnic, political, and ideological viewpoints they would have rarely, if ever, seen on network or cable news programs. I was extremely proud of the outcome of the panel discussion and can only hope mainstream media heads noted the value of bringing diverse voices to the table to discuss issues that affect all Americans.

It's not that I have abandoned my commitment to the concerns of Black people. Hardly. Everywhere I go, I bring my whole self with me; which means everywhere I go, I bring my Blackness with me. My love for Black people will never, ever go away.

To the contrary, the evolution I describe is more about embracing the totality of Dr. King's message. He, too, started with a particular love for Black people but went on to propagate a universal love that embraced all humanity.

My love of humanity starts unapologetically with my people because I understand our struggle, which continues to this very day. But on the battlefield of race and class, injustice and exclusion, Black people are not exclusive targets.

It is the memory of Dr. King that encourages me to sound the clarion call for political accountability. Too many conversations revolve around the concerns of the rich and lucky or the so-called middle class. Few talk about the poor, the disenfranchised, or the underprivileged. The "haves" get attention, while the "have-nots" languish out of sight.

Too many Americans keep insisting that we must "take our country back." They yearn for the "good ol' days," forgetting (or ignoring) that those days weren't so good for red, Black, and brown folk. Others are boiling mad over immigration. It's a waste of energy. No fence, no wall, no amount of troops along the border will ever dim the constitutional promise of liberty, freedom, and opportunity for all. Let's face it: No one's going anywhere!

In 2010, *Forbes* magazine cited U.S. Census figures to make the argument that diversity needs to be a high priority in this country. By the year 2050, racial/ethnic minorities (Latinos at 30 percent, African Americans at 12 percent, and Asian Americans at 8 percent) will comprise 55 percent of America's working-age population. In a world where China and India are superpowers and the marketplace is global, we need to prepare a cadre of colorful emissaries to help this country remain relevant in the 21st century and beyond.

Dr. King's operational definition of love means that everyone is worthy—just because. It's not about titles, wealth, or skin color. LOVE means everyone is worthy—just because.

A similar theme was found in the 2005 editorial, "How the Civil Rights Movement affected U.S. immigration," published by the Sound Vision Foundation, a nonprofit religious organization dedicated to producing constructive and educational Islamic media content.

Beginning with the familiar words, "Give me your tired, your poor, your huddled masses yearning to breathe free," the commentary reads: "Until the 1960s, this famous inscription which is found on the Statue of Liberty in New York Harbor—the site where many immigrants arrived in America in the early 20th century—applied only to whites. But thanks to the country's Civil Rights Movement, among other factors, immigrants of all colors were welcomed into the country."

This civil rights emphasis on human rights brought world attention to America's exclusion of all nonwhite immigrants, the commentary stresses. Discriminatory laws that restricted the freedoms of Black people also stifled the ambitions of darker-skinned immigrants, women, Hispanics, Asians, lesbians, gays, and transgendered; they served to choke off basic human rights for all Americans.

The Foundation elaborated, adding that "America's Muslims are enjoying the fruits of the struggle as well," and "many of the Muslims who came to study, work, and later establish their families in this country could simply not have done so had U.S. immigration laws retained their discriminatory nature."

As I've frequently said and written: When we make Black America better, we make all of America better. No matter what nation we call home, all of us celebrate our true humanity when the least of us are economically, socially, and spiritually uplifted.

*Justice for all*
*Service to others*
*Love that liberates*

This is the diversity imperative that will truly make America a nation as good as its promise.

## TAVIS'S TAKEAWAY:

Justice for all, service to others, and a love that liberates.

© Courtesy of the Tavis Smiley Collection

# CHAPTER 14

# SAVE SPACE
# FOR GRACE

The phone call came every year for 15 years: "I know your life is moving along, but I know you, Tavis. I know you are not feeling complete about this. You've got to finish. If not, it's going to come back to haunt you one day."

It was Ms. Dorothy, my counselor from Indiana University. She knew that I had left the university in my senior year without completing my degree. Ms. Dorothy had been keeping up with my career. Even though I was on national radio and TV, she worried that one day my reputation might be damaged if it were ever discovered that I hadn't "officially" graduated.

"I don't want you lying," Ms. Dorothy usually continued. "We can do it by correspondence, but

I want you to finish. You're too close, and your future is so promising."

Fortunately, I hadn't told any lies. Interviewers didn't probe the "attended Indiana University" line on my résumé. My ascension in media was based on previous jobs. I went from local media to national media in steady succession.

Yet Ms. Dorothy did indeed know me. I didn't feel complete without the degree. Not because I didn't have it, but the reason why I didn't have it was what bothered me. I paid a huge penalty for backing someone into a corner and failing to save space for grace.

## Finishing the Task

> *"Once a task you have first begun,*
> *never finish until it is done.*
> *Be the labor great or small,*
> *do it well or not at all."*

> — BIG MAMA

I intended to follow Big Mama's sage advice, but the "labor" was indeed great.

As my three-month internship in Los Angeles came to a close, I found myself deeply in love with the city. I started telling friends I wasn't going back to Indiana. I'd transfer to UCLA, USC, or anywhere in California to finish my senior year.

Somehow, Mayor Bradley got wind of my plans. He called me into his office:

"Tavis, you're going to go back to school, and you are going to get that degree," he said resolutely. "If I had known that this internship would cause you to not finish your education, I wouldn't have let you come."

The mayor didn't completely burst my bubble though. He offered a deal: Once I finished my education at Indiana, he'd have a job waiting for me after graduation. How could I refuse? There weren't many of my classmates who had a prestigious job lined up a year before they graduated.

I went back to Indiana—begrudgingly. After my internship in fast-paced LA, Bloomington seemed as slow as frozen molasses. My parents, who I always believed would grow old together, were embroiled in a bitter divorce. I was burnt-out, tired, and depressed, but determined to finish the task.

My mood was already sour the day one of my teachers popped a quiz on her students. The classroom wasn't your typical, spacious lecture hall; it was so small that the hundred or so students could barely turn without bumping noses.

Two days later, the teacher returned our graded papers. I missed only one or two questions, but there was a circled, red "F" at the top of my paper, with a handwritten message from the teacher: "Next time, keep your eyes on your own paper."

I hadn't cheated. I was livid.

"What is the meaning of this?" I stood and shouted.

"It's self-explanatory," she quipped; "keep your eyes on your own paper."

Oh, it was so on!

With my honed debating skills, I reamed her. Like F. Lee Bailey or Johnnie Cochran, I relentlessly deconstructed her defenses. She insisted she saw me cheating. How is that possible? We were packed in the classroom like sardines! How could she tell who was cheating or who was simply turning their heads? If I supposedly cheated, I argued, she was obligated to call me out at that time, not two days later.

"Who else cheated?" I spat. "For all I know, you could have just picked me out for other reasons and given me an 'F' to justify your biases."

"W-w-what do you mean?" the teacher stammered.

"What part do you not understand? I'm the only Black person in this class."

She stammered, broke into tears, and grabbed her things as she dismissed the class and bolted out of the room.

Perhaps I was taking my frustrations out on that teacher. Although she certainly deserved to be checked, I left no wiggle room for a graceful retreat.

If I had, maybe it wouldn't have taken me 16 years to get my degree.

# What Goes Around . . .

There was no reprimand for my outburst. In fact, after hearing both sides, the dean told the teacher that she hadn't handled the situation correctly. If I had cheated, she was obligated to inform me at that time. He made the teacher restore my grade.

After the humiliated teacher left his office, the dean asked that I stay behind.

"I highly recommend you switch out of that class," he said. "I have the feeling this tension is not going to get any better. This course is a requirement for you to graduate. Don't put yourself in a bad situation."

Feeling highly justified, I thanked the dean for his advice but insisted I had done nothing wrong and didn't plan to drop the class. She was wrong, not me. If anybody should drop the class, it should be the teacher, I insisted.

The rest of that semester was torture. I had an internship in the chancellor's office, debate team duties, and several other challenging classes; the conflict between my mother and father also unsettled me. I was bored with the class in which I had the confrontation, and I skipped the majority of those classes.

At semester's end I was in trouble. I absolutely had to pass the student teacher's class to graduate. Since I skipped the class, I knew none of the material. The course was a requirement, but all I needed was a pass/fail grade. In other words, a "D-" would do. I sweated through long nights of intense study to get ready.

I took the test and flunked it. Miserably.

Now I was backed into a corner. I had to go see the teacher and share my woeful tale. I told her about the job waiting for me in California that I just couldn't miss. I begged her to let me take another exam or make it up in some way.

"Is there anything you can do?" I pleaded.

"Anything I can do?" she said, unmoved, defiantly looking into my eyes.

"Why, Mr. Smiley, surely you're not asking me to inflate your grade? You of all people aren't asking me to give you a grade you didn't earn?"

She took so much joy and delight in the turned tables. I can't say I blamed her. The first week of the semester, I got her in trouble. The last week, there I was—in trouble—begging her for a "D-," anything but another big, fat "F."

Apparently done with the conversation and me, the teacher pointed to my test paper: "This is what you got. This is the way it's going to be. Sorry, can't help you. Bye, bye."

## Thank You, Ms. Dorothy

Luckily, I had enough credit hours to participate in the graduation ceremony that May. At least I could look like I was graduating on time. My entire family came to the ceremony, but I didn't have the courage to tell them I hadn't actually completed my degree. I'd have to deal with that unfinished business later. In California. Mayor Bradley was expecting me to start on a certain date, and I was determined to show up for work on that day.

After arriving in LA, to my surprise and disappointment, I had to wait more than a year to rejoin the mayor's staff. I was stuck in California hustling just to eat and pay rent. Going to summer school to earn the credits I needed to get my degree was impossible.

The mayor's staff assumed I had a degree. But over the years, the guilt was eating at me. I attended my siblings' college graduations, knowing that neither they nor Mama and Dad were aware that I wasn't a certified graduate. What made this all so ironic was that I was the one paying most of the bills for my younger siblings to attend college, and they had degrees conferred on them while I had still not completed all of my course requirements! Interestingly, I had received a number of awards and recognitions from colleges and universities for my societal contributions before I had secured my bachelor's degree in public policy from Indiana! But even the high honor of being recognized by some of the nation's top schools didn't alleviate my guilt of not having completed the requirements to graduate.

But what really got to me even more was Ms. Dorothy. She called again, 15 years after I had left Indiana, to say she planned to retire that year:

"I do not intend to retire without you having your degree," she said.

That was it. I made arrangements to complete my studies from Los Angeles. When I finished the course work months later, I was told the degree would be mailed to my home.

Dr. Kenneth R. R. Gros Louis, the chancellor I interned with in my final year at Indiana, had a summer home in Santa Barbara, California. One day, he called and asked if I could meet him for lunch while he was on the West Coast. At the conclusion of our lunch, Dr. Gros Louis said he had something for me. He stood, reached into his briefcase, pulled out my degree, cleared his throat, and . . . well, he described it best in the March/April 2004 edition of *Indiana Alumni Magazine*:

"I said, 'By the authority vested in me, through the president and the board of trustees, I'm pleased to confer upon you your degree.' And he got quite teary. He didn't cry, but it was a much more emotional moment than I thought it was going to be. It was a nice meeting and a long conversation, and I was very impressed with his intelligence—and always have been—but also the warmth of his personality."

After Dr. Gros Louis gave his formal conferral presentation, people started clapping, I started crying—it was a delightful, emotional moment on a beautiful day in sunny Southern California.

*Indiana Alumni Magazine* did the cover story with a picture of me holding my newly conferred degree. The caption read: "Tavis Smiley finally gets his degree 16 years later." I sent it to my parents. Albeit 16 years later, they finally learned their son was indeed a college graduate.

## So Right Can Be So Wrong

We've all encountered people who push our buttons. They wrong us, insult us, and sometimes embarrass us in public. Their comeuppance is deserved, we rationalize. If they push, we can feel perfectly justified in pushing back in kind, right?

Maybe not, especially when we consider the consequences.

Sometimes you can be so right and so wrong at the same time. Millions of Americans have lost their jobs in the past few years. I'm sure some who were unceremoniously escorted off the job felt justifiably betrayed, demeaned, or humiliated. Wars start because leaders often leave no room for compromise and their opponents have no graceful exit. Many individuals in relationships who feel wronged or abandoned react violently, and too many kids use guns to settle perceived disrespect.

Yet the way we leave our last job affects how we get the next one. Payback may feel great at the time, but as my situation demonstrated, what goes around sometimes comes back around. There are better ways to diffuse volatile situations than humiliating an adversary. Instead of excoriating the teacher in front of the class, I should have gone straight to the dean. As a third party, he could have helped us respectfully detach from our emotions.

In the CBS.MoneyWatch article, "Laid Off? 7 Rules for a Graceful Exit," Amy Levin-Epstein offers useful tips that apply outside of job-loss situations. She suggests we avoid taking slights personally, remain cool in confrontational situations, and find "safe places" with therapists or friends where we can discuss feelings of humiliation, shame, and terror.

Sometimes our anger isn't even about the circumstance. The offending party may have tapped into negative past experiences. With the teacher, I sensed racial bias. That could have been more about me than her.

Psychologists and sociologists recommend that we try to leave room for analysis—examine the motivators that fuel the event. As with any good relationship, sometimes we have to compromise, even surrender. Be it on the job, in the home, or someplace else—sometimes being right can be detrimentally wrong.

I learned the hard way that the price paid for blind retribution can come back on you. As I've grown over the years, I've tried not to put people on the spot or back them into corners of no retreat. But honestly, it's been challenging.

An interview on my old BET show comes to mind. The guest was a celebrity whom I respect tremendously. But I was on edge during the conversation. In her book, the artist wrote that she'd rather be called a "bitch or a ho"—anything but "African-American." She was not a hyphenation, the author insisted: She was just an "American."

Her position, from my perspective, was wrong and insulting to Black people. During our back-and-forth discussion on the show, I said, "You can't be serious!"

"I am serious. How do I know I'm from Africa? I could be from . . . say . . . Egypt."

WHAT?!

Everything in me wanted to say: You do know that Egypt is in Africa, don't you?

I didn't.

I reminded myself: Even when you're right and they're wrong, don't pounce.

We took a commercial break, and her handlers rushed over immediately to point out her egregious error. After coming back on the air, we continued talking about the book, never returning to the Egypt comment. Restraint was the order of that day. She got the point without being publicly challenged. Thankfully, I rejected the impulse to pounce.

We are still friends to this day.

A relationship was maintained because I had learned how to save space for grace.

## TAVIS'S TAKEAWAY:

Don't "give" grace;
allow grace to give.

© Courtesy of the Tavis Smiley Collection

# CHAPTER 15

# AND THE WINNER IS …NOT ME

"I can't stand here tonight and say it doesn't hurt."

It was 9:50 P.M., Tuesday, November 4, 1980. Standing before supporters inside the Sheraton Washington Hotel, President Jimmy Carter delivered one of the earliest presidential concession speeches in history. The nation's 39th President had a difficult time containing his emotions. He had suffered a crushing defeat by Ronald Wilson Reagan. With an approval rating of just over 30 percent, Carter's loss meant that he would join Herbert Hoover as the only other elected incumbent ousted by voters.

I've interviewed many important people over the years, but the time I've spent with Carter has served as a powerful reminder that truth and goodness are much greater than money and power. In his book, *The Unfinished Presidency*, author Douglas Brinkley hints at why the Georgia peanut farmer was destined to become a one-term president:

> *"Carter never fit in the capital*
> *because his leadership style was essentially*
> *religious in nature, more preacher than politician.*
> *Among American presidents only Carter peppered his*
> *speeches with the word 'love' and earnest Christian*
> *entreaties for 'tenderness' and 'healing' . . .*
> *Carter was a 'wheeler-healer' who simply*
> *refused to become a 'wheeler-dealer.'"*

After leaving the White House, the wheeler-healer used his influence to promote peace and justice around the globe. He won the Nobel Peace Prize in 2002. When announcing the award, the Norwegian Nobel Committee cited the ex-President's decades of "untiring effort to find peaceful solutions to international conflicts, to advance democracy and human rights, and to promote economic and social development."

The universe, sometimes without our knowledge, fails us at critical junctures in order to nudge us toward our destinies. Carter's rejection by the voters—his loss to Reagan—was in some ways a win for humankind. His post-presidency mission echoes a truism that I have come to adore: "We plan and God laughs." In Carter, we are reminded that sometimes rejection is really purposeful redirection.

## Champing at the Bit

Folks who really knew me as a kid will recall how I used to brag about one day becoming the first Black U.S. Senator from Indiana. The embers were stoked in my teenage years when I served as an assistant for Councilman Douglas Hogan, a Black man with authentic passion for his job. Hogan asked me—at the age of 16—to join him at a Democratic fundraiser, where I sat next to U.S. Senator Birch Bayh, Indiana's most prominent politician. I lit up when the Senator shared his thoughts on Dr. King and the nobility of public service.

Those political embers were sparked as a result of my internship with Bloomington's Mayor Allison. They burst into flames after my joining Los Angeles Mayor Tom Bradley's staff, first as an intern, then, two years later, as Bradley's administrative aide.

Back then and even more so now, I placed public servants on the same tier as schoolteachers. Both are noble professions. I'm not talking about your garden variety, "me first" politician; I mean those, like Councilman Hogan who, above all else, put people first. There's also something sacred about people giving you their money, their vote, their time, and their trust. By these actions they say: "We entrust our future to you. Where you lead, we will follow."

That sacred trust should never be taken for granted.

Bradley was an attentive and effective mayor. He was able to serve all corners of LA by dividing it into eight sections and assigning aides to serve as his eyes, ears, and voice in each of those sections. In this role, I was the pseudo-deputy mayor of South LA.

As the mayor's go-to guy, I met a whole lot of voters, made friends, and developed valuable connections. Perhaps I was a bit ambitious, but after only three years with Bradley, I decided to enter the political arena as a candidate. The 6th Council District seat was up for grabs. The district, at the time, was split—half Black, half white basically. I felt the councilwoman representing the district served her white constituents pretty well, but I can't say the same about how she served her Black constituents. I honestly believed I'd be a better public servant who would represent all citizens with equal amounts of energy, vigor, and focus.

Of course my peers in the mayor's office ridiculed me relentlessly: "Who does Tavis think he is? He's only been here three years and now he's running for office"—the usual negatives that flow from the jealous and the fearful. Most everyone, including the mayor, warned me that I was making a huge mistake. Some pointed out that I was putting the mayor in an awkward position. The incumbent wasn't particularly an enemy of the mayor's, and he needed her vote on a number of important issues. People feared that, by association, it would be assumed that the mayor had endorsed his assistant's campaign.

He didn't. He let me know that he couldn't endorse me.

What Bradley did do, however, was tell his campaign treasurer to work with me and provide access to all his fundraising contacts. In one sense, the mayor's campaign guy became my campaign guy, which helped me raise a lot of money and gain more support.

I ran a spirited campaign, a good campaign, a clean campaign.

I lost.

I came in third place.

Many people run for office just to get their name out in public. Not me. I wanted to win. I wanted to serve. But timing was my enemy. Most folks simply thought it wasn't my time. I was young, I'd get another shot, they figured. Others believed it was best not to make enemies and to stick with the incumbent.

I took the loss very personally. Not only was my political fire doused, I also felt the voters had rejected me as a public servant. The path I had passionately trod since boyhood had suddenly vanished.

# Getting Your Hustle On!

Hustle was the order of the days that followed my political defeat. I was flat broke.

Again.

But this time, with a huge campaign debt over my head. I had left the mayor's office to run for the council. Not only did I lose the election, I lost a steady paycheck as well. It was back to my days of sardines and crackers and a regimen of hustle, hustle, and more hustle.

Actor Will Smith has been a guest on my programs many times. I will never forget the interview in which he defined his recipe for success:

"Tavis, I'm not the smartest, not the most handsome—although I do think I'm kinda cute—and I'm not the best actor. I'm the first to tell you all that and then some. But let me tell you this: I will never, ever be out-worked. You will not out-work me or out-hustle me."

Smith, one of the number-one box office stars in the world, underscored the secret of survival after loss. Refusing to be out-hustled, out-strategized, or out-worked is the stuff that makes the difference.

Alexander Graham Bell added another survival tip: "When one door closes, another door opens; but we often look so long and so regretfully upon the closed door, that we do not see the ones which open for us."

So after I licked my wounds, I hustled toward those yet-unopened doors.

Although I didn't run for office to get my name out in public, I knew how important it was to keep it there. My background thus far had prepared me for my core strengths—debating, politics, and public speaking. LA was a big market, but there weren't any young, Black, insightful, and well-informed commentators on the air. I set my sights on radio.

The election was in May; by November, I had a gig on a local Los Angeles radio station. I've detailed the timeline in other chapters of this book. Here, I'll just summarize: That local radio job led to bigger local offers, which led to local TV, and later, to other opportunities that took me outside of LA's boundaries and onto the national media stage.

The point of this playback is to underscore the opportunity to use rejection as a launching pad and recognize the importance of links. When faced with failed endeavors or job loss, you don't have to know the exact steps to rebound, but it does help to know what opportunities link to your strengths. The opportunities may not pay much money, but they may further your new direction.

I was a pre-law/public policy major, not a communications guy. Neither media nor journalism was my field of study. But I was fortunate enough to create opportunities that linked to my core strengths. That placed me on a path that led to my being on national TV and radio and writing best-selling books. This was not what I expected. It was the blessing that came from rejection.

## You Can't Dictate the Journey

The Bible says, in Romans 8:28, that "all things work together for good to those who love God and are called according to His purpose." Note that the scripture doesn't say: "all things are going to be good." It says all things "work for" your good.

I think this applies to everyone—believer or not—because, ultimately, everything in life is a learning experience. When things don't work out the way you want them to, remember: Sometimes a dead end is in fact a finish line. Maybe the universe has prepared you for another race.

Perception is an important factor in assessing your chances for success. I explored this topic on my TV program with Maria Bartiromo. There will be times in your life when you're down and out. Bartiromo, who interviewed dozens of successful people for her book, stresses that the "down and out" period is the best time to define your future:

"It's exactly this time—when things are troubled and you're struggling and you're not sure when it's gonna end—that you actually find the tools to strengthen and rise above it and succeed," Bartiromo told me, adding that successful people share a similar experience:

"I learned that one thing that they had in common, everyone that I spoke with . . . walked away feeling smarter—not during the peaks in their careers, but the valleys in their careers."

In my case, I discovered that rejection was really a new direction. I was downcast when I wasn't elected a public servant. But when you think about it, I am a public servant. What I do now is public service—literally and figuratively; I'm on public radio and public TV. My platforms allow me to introduce Americans to each other; challenge them to reexamine the assumptions they hold; and help them to expand their inventory of ideas.

In what direction would my life have gone had I been elected to the city council? I used to think about that all the time. There have been at least two occasions when the powers that be have approached me about running for an open seat in Congress from California. If I had accepted their offer, perhaps I could have been a member of the United States Congress.

But then what?

In the political arena, there's no way I could have established the platforms that I have doing what I love to do every day. As a broadcaster, I am unencumbered by the responsibilities of raising millions to be reelected, paying back political favors and swallowing compromises that betray my values. I am blessed with a rare level of independence, and when politicians or other notables want to get their positions or projects out to the public, they ask to be on my shows.

I've never dictated the journey. And, as we can see, God had a far better plan for me.

The key to success is self-knowledge and developing a vision of your life that inspires you. This, too, was something I discussed with Bartiromo. In her book, she poignantly observed that "Dr. King never said, 'I have a business plan.' He said, 'I have a dream.'

"We want a dream and we want a vision, but we want that vision built on solid ground. We want to know that it's realistic," Bartiromo continued. "So the first law of success is knowing yourself. Self-knowledge. Know what you can do. Know where your love is and what you have in your belly, that fire in your belly, to actually do well. Once you have a clear picture of who you are, what you can accomplish, where you'd like to go, you can start actually putting a vision together to get there."

To "get there," it is so vitally important that we keep rejection in proper perspective. Actor, director, and producer Sylvester Stallone put it this way: "I take rejection as someone blowing a bugle in my ear to wake me up and get going, rather than to retreat."

The way life has unfolded, I'm now much more comfortable when things don't go the way I think they're supposed to. Experience has schooled me well. Now, when my friends call me to complain about not getting this or missing out on that opportunity, I listen intently, but inevitably I encourage them to consider the possibility that their desires weren't aligned with their destinies. Or, as best-selling author James Lee Burke phrases it: "There's nothing like rejection to make you do an inventory of yourself."

I never minimize their frustrations or disappointments. Whatever advice or encouragement I give, it circles back to the underlying theme of this chapter:

"We plan and God laughs."

## TAVIS'S TAKEAWAY:

Rejection is
re-direction.

© Courtesy of the Tavis Smiley Collection

# CHAPTER 16

# KEEP IT TIGHT

"He was a rock star. I remember being in Athens with him; everybody coming down the path would stop and talk to him and say, 'Aren't you Tom Bradley?'"

Bee Lavery, Mayor Bradley's chief of protocol, captured his essence perfectly. A Los Angeles icon, the mayor was beloved by many. It wasn't just because he showed LA how to rise above its racial animosity during his two campaigns in 1969 and 1973. His administration gave the city a much-needed, progressive facelift, but that wasn't the sum total of Mayor Bradley's legacy either. Winning the rights to host the 1984 Olympic Games and pulling off a successful, surplus-producing event was a major accomplishment; but even that didn't completely encompass the full range of his "rock star" standing.

In Hollywood, looks can carry a person a long way. And Mr. Mayor—the tall, statuesque, former UCLA track star and former police commander—had the "look," the vitality, fitness, and charisma of an LA mayor. This is in no way to diminish his unprecedented political contributions, but, like Bee Lavery, I served with the man. I saw how people, especially women, responded to his presence. It was through him that I learned an important maxim: "If you want to be perceived as a sharp and smart individual, you have to live and dress the part."

The "Bradley way" was on my mind when my ex-boss called and asked to have lunch with me. This was long after he had left office and I was hosting my show on BET. I knew he was proud of me; after all, I was the ambitious kid he tapped to intern for him and later hired as his assistant. He watched me pull myself up after I left his administration and unsuccessfully ran for a Los Angeles city council seat. My shields were lowered when we sat down for lunch. So I was stunned by his opening salvo:

"Tavis, you've gotten too big."

## All Things Considered . . .

The mayor didn't mean "big" as in big-headed celebrity big. He straight out told me I had gotten too fat. Which was true. I was carrying about 70 pounds too much. I started packing on the weight after three basketball- and tennis-related injuries.

Over the course of three years, I had lateral meniscus tears in both knees and tore the Achilles tendon in my right foot. In between rehabbing and recuperating from those injuries and surgeries, I had gained 70 pounds. As a result, my back hurt, I had trouble breathing, and I suffered from sleep apnea—everything that comes along with being overweight. That was tough for me; I had been skinny most of my life.

It was in my grossly overweight phase that Mayor Bradley called. Of course, he was unaware of my injuries. He just turned on BET, saw his bloated former intern on the air, and, I suppose, decided it was time to arrange a one-on-one intervention.

This elder statesman was always a man of few words, so he wasted not one syllable when addressing me:

"Tavis, I don't want to preach to you, but I've found this to be true in my 80 years of living, and I want you to always remember this: All other things being equal—and do not forget the first part of this formulation," he stressed; "all other things being equal, the person who looks the best—9.9 times out of 10—will always win.

"If two people are applying for a job and have the exact same qualifications except one is overweight and sloppy, and the other is lean and well-groomed, the more fit person will most always win."

If I didn't get the weight off and keep it off, my former boss insisted, I was going to lose—not based on intellect— "you'll always have that," he added, but on "aesthetics."

"You have always been on top of your game, and I don't ever want to see you lose," he continued in a fatherly tone. "Remember, all other things being equal . . . you have to keep it tight, keep it tight, Tavis."

## Remembering Bradley

Not long after our meeting, Tom Bradley suffered a heart attack and, later, a stroke that left him partially paralyzed and unable to speak for the remainder of his life. Two years after our luncheon, Tom Bradley passed away at the age of 80.

That luncheon stays with me, not necessarily because of what the mayor said; it was the way he expressed concern for my health and career. The mayor and ex-police commander rarely talked to me on a personal level like he did at that luncheon. I felt the love and genuine concern in his admonition. This was a man who wanted me to continue to be a winner. His point was well taken—"all things being equal . . .": I had to get myself in shape.

I hired a trainer and went to work on losing those 70 pounds. With my tendency toward overcompensation, I completed three marathons, despite my trainer's warnings.

Of course, I broke my left foot at mile 20 of my first 26.2-mile marathon, but, hey, I finished the race. I have stayed on a regimen designed to keep my weight under control, although it remains a daily struggle.

During our luncheon, Mayor Bradley made a convincing "win or lose" argument. However, today, on a larger societal scale, it's no longer about keeping your weight down simply to advance your career; it's about advancing your life.

## From Win or Lose to Life or Death

Staying tight, keeping fit is not just about winning or losing a job as Mayor Bradley stressed. Today, it's a life-or-death reality.

According to NetWellness, a nonprofit consumer health Website, some of the most serious diseases and causes of death for Blacks like me include diabetes, heart disease, most forms of cancer, stroke, and AIDS. African Americans tend to develop high blood pressure at younger ages than other groups, and Blacks—both men and women—suffer disproportionately from a variety of cancers as compared to whites.

While it's no laughing matter, my friend the comedian, George Wallace, jokes that he doesn't understand why Black men even have to pay into social security, since we're not going to be around long enough to collect anyway!

We also have the highest obesity rates, with 37 percent of Black men and nearly 50 percent of Black women topping out the category. Hispanic and Black children also have higher rates of childhood diabetes than white children.

Too many kids, especially Black and Latino kids, are grossly overweight. Recent data from the Centers for Disease Control show that 20 percent of African American and Hispanic children ages 2 to 19 are obese versus 15 percent of white children. Experts say that the growth of obesity and childhood Type 2 diabetes in the past 10 or 20 years is directly related to sedentary lifestyles, video games, and junk food consumption.

"The introduction of computers, hand-held and video games has had an alarming effect on children," says Megann Dastrup, a Verde Valley Medical Center dietician, in an article "Poor Diet and Sedentary Lifestyle Linked to Childhood Diabetes." Being inside and inactive, sitting in front of televisions or computers, watching fast-food commercials that trigger desires to eat fast and fatty foods are all complicit in the web of lifestyle choices that lead to premature death.

The personal struggle to overcome my own weight problems has turned into a public, anti-obesity advocacy campaign. I have been drawn onto the battlefield with those fighting other deadly diseases that disproportionately impact African Americans and send them to early graves. It's impossible to number the health fairs I've hosted, attended, or sponsored.

A permanent fixture in my outreach efforts are the "Road to Health" seminars and segments on my PBS show.

The issue is very important to me. In my mind, success in politics, entertainment, or the media means absolutely nothing if politicians, actors, or media folk don't use their power and platforms to improve the lives of their constituents and audiences.

Take Al Roker of the *Today* show as an example. Before undergoing gastric bypass surgery in 2002, he weighed in at an astonishing 320 pounds. Someone dear to Roker asked that he lose some weight. Unlike the advice I received from Mayor Bradley, the request Roker received came during a hospital visit with his father, Al Roker, Sr., who was dying from cancer.

In 2010, he told his colleagues about a hospital visit in 2001 where he was with his Dad, who said there was something very important he needed to share with his eldest son. He knew his time was short. Roker recalled that day with his Dad, a long-time New York City bus driver: "He said to me: 'Look. You've got to promise me that you're going to lose weight. We both know I'm not going to be here to help you with my grandchildren. So you've got to promise me.'"

Al made the promise.

That evening his father lost the ability to speak. Three weeks later he passed away.

The TV weatherman has kept his word. And to this day, he credits his dying father's last wish for motivating him to tackle his obesity problem. Al lost nearly 140 pounds and 20 suit sizes. Yes, there was a slight relapse, but when he told the story in June 2010, he weighed in at an impressive 204 pounds.

Equally impressive is the 2007 documentary on childhood obesity that he produced for the Food Network: *Childhood Obesity: Danger Zone*. The 57-year-old NBC personality used his own experience and battles with weight control to explore the serious weight problems and the health risks more than 12 million obese American children and teenagers face every day.

First Lady Michelle Obama has also contributed significantly to the effort by launching her "Let's Move" anti-obesity campaign in early 2010. Her goal of ending "the epidemic of childhood obesity in a generation" is indeed ambitious but doable, with government resources also aimed at the problem.

Addressing obesity is going to take more than telling people to eat less and eat healthier. The nation needs to step up and address the fact that most low-income areas don't have full-service grocery stores. Residents in these neighborhoods depend on gas stations and convenience stores, where, as noted in an article in *The Christian Science Monitor* that discussed Mrs. Obama's efforts, "The only thing that's crisp and green is the money" poor people put in the proprietors' cash registers.

In an attempt to address the healthy food scarcity problem, President Obama has proposed $400 million in his fiscal year 2011 budget to help bring grocery stores to underserved urban and rural areas and to help neighborhood stores carry healthier items.

The Obamas are superstars, especially in Black households most principally because of the historic roles they play as President and First Lady. But also because, let's face it, they do look good! His nicotine habit notwithstanding, the Obamas have committed themselves and their family to eating healthy and staying fit. In other words, they keep it tight.

Remember, "all other things being equal . . ." I think you get it.

**TAVIS'S TAKEAWAY:**

Eat to live,
not live to eat.

© Courtesy of the Tavis Smiley Collection

**CHAPTER 17**

# GET READY
# TO BE READY

It was the chance of a lifetime. The opportunity arose for me to jump from a voice on the radio to a face on the local news. Most of my friends were ecstatic about the possibilities, not to mention the increase in my salary. I'd be a fool to say no, they said.

I said "no."

It was a huge mistake, according to some in my circle. Mistake though it might have been, without this seeming failure to take advantage of a once-in-a-lifetime opportunity, I would have never been able to fail up. Nor would I have had time to discover the true meaning of defining your own success.

# No Thanks, Not Yet

When I lost my bid for the 6th District city council seat, I entertained the idea of running again in four years. Why not? I ran a spirited campaign, received a healthy share of the votes, and developed a cadre of powerful and active supporters. Mayor Bradley lost his first run for his seat in 1969, so the second time might have been the charm for me, too.

However, if one loses a political race and seriously intends to run for that office again, there are at least three things he or she might want to accomplish first:

1. Make some money to live on and to pay off any debt from the previous campaign.

2. Find something that's going to keep your name in the public eye.

3. Find something that will allow you to be vocal about issues that matter to voters.

In order to address all three tasks, I managed to land a gig with a small, Black-owned radio station where I delivered 60-second commentaries. I became adept at delivering *The Smiley Report*—one-minute commentaries with a beginning, middle, and end.

The segment was so well received during afternoon drive-time that the station owner gave me a second airing in the morning. I was heard at 7:20 in the morning and again at 5:20 in the afternoon. I didn't make any real money, but my name and voice were out there, talking about issues that mattered to voters.

The show was on an AM radio station with a limited audience. But it became so popular I was able to transition to the FM side with a bigger listenership. The jump came courtesy of the genius Stevie Wonder, who owns an FM radio station based in LA. After a few years with Stevie, the #1 urban station in LA asked if I'd be a part of its lineup. The offer was too big to refuse; it also had a much wider broadcast signal that was heard in and well outside of LA.

As the story goes, Terry Crofoot, the general manager at KABC-TV, picked up his kids after school every day. As with so many other white, suburban kids, Crofoot's children were fascinated with Black music. Every day they'd switch his radio dial to the more hip station—the urban station that broadcast my daily commentaries. Thanks to his kids, my commentaries caught Crofoot's attention.

KABC-TV was the only station in LA with personalities who delivered commentaries live every evening. The commentators it employed—three women and two men—were all white. One of them, Bruce Herschensohn, had announced his departure in order to challenge Barbara Boxer for the U.S. Senate seat. The job was so prestigious that several commentators used it to advance their careers, including famed attorney Gloria Allred and former California Senator John V. Tunney.

Crofoot told his news director, Roger Bell, about my radio commentaries. Bell called to ask if I'd be interested in auditioning for a commentator position.

I was in my late 20s, with the largest urban radio station in the city, and now I had the opportunity to add "television" commentator to my portfolio. My friends were jumping up and down with excitement. It was my "moment," some said.

"Thank you, but no thank you," I told Bell when I called him back.

Many of my friends thought I was nuts. Who in their right mind passes up an opportunity that had gained others so much exposure?

In truth, I turned it down because I wasn't ready. I had never done television, never used a TelePrompTer, and never spoken before a television camera. It was indeed a once-in-a-lifetime opportunity. But I was convinced that if I went in and bombed the audition, the word might get out that I was good on radio but horrible on television. In my state of mind at the time, I felt bombing might foreclose on any future television opportunities.

When I told Bell "no thanks," I was really thinking "not yet."

## Preparation, Preparation, and More Preparation

Days after declining Bell's offer, I went to a little community TV outlet called South Central Community Television (SCCT) on Crenshaw Boulevard. The staff knew me from radio and were ecstatic that I wanted to do commentary for free. It wasn't about the money. It was about experience, learning the ins and outs of television commentary.

At SCCT I learned how to write my scripts, read a prompter without turning my head from side to side, give the right inflection, sit upright in my chair, and tuck my jacket under my butt to prevent ripples across my shoulders—all the TV tricks.

After about eight months with the small cable outlet, I still felt unprepared. When I was in college, I remembered meeting a big-time Montreal TV producer, Larry Shapiro, who created content for PBS. I called Larry and asked if he could teach me a few things about working in front of and behind the camera.

"I don't have a whole lot of money, but I can get you a little apartment here in Montreal and pay you a little bit," Larry graciously responded. "You can come up here for a year, and I'll teach you everything you need to know about TV. And once you get good enough, I'll even let you host a couple of my shows for PBS."

I was in Montreal in a flash. For almost a year, Larry taught me how to sell advertising and to work with multiple cameras; what the duties of a "floor director" are; and—keeping his word—eventually let me host a couple of his shows. Who knew that, years later, I'd end up as the first person of color in the history of PBS to host his own daily signature talk show?

I returned to LA ready to take KABC's offer. But would there still be an offer?

"Hey, Tavis; surprised to hear from you. Haven't heard you on the radio for awhile."

I simply told him that I'd been busy before. Then I asked him if he had filled the commentator slot.

"As a matter of fact, we haven't," Bell answered. "Why don't you come on in tomorrow, and we'll do a quick test."

It was close to 3:30 in the afternoon when I arrived for my audition at the TV station. News anchors were in the area preparing to go on the air; a year prior, I would have been intimidated by their presence. But now, I felt like I knew exactly what I was doing.

I sat confidently at the anchor's desk. I was handed a mock script. The camera swung toward me. The green light flashed. The director shouted: "Action!"

One take. I nailed it.

The gawking anchors were aghast. Roger Bell walked over, shocked:

"I called you over a year ago and you were this good?"

I started the following week; and every week for a couple of years, I was a commentator on the five o'clock news.

My friends were right: The job quickly opened other doors. After being on TV, KABC Talk Radio—the #1 talk radio station—wanted me to do commentary for it. That eventually morphed into my own talk show with the company.

Frank Sinatra once said, "Never ignore that inner voice that tells you something can be better, even when everybody tells you it's okay."

While my friends were warning me that turning down KABC-TV's offer was a big mistake, my inner voice whispered: "Get prepared first!"

## Stay Ready to Be Ready

This particular "mistake" had a good—no, great—outcome. I share it because it contains layers of valuable lessons. The first pertains to preparation. There's so much mediocrity in society because people oftentimes jump before they're ready. Nobody wants to miss what he or she perceives as an opportunity, but very few take the time to prepare for it.

My grandfather used to say: "Son, if you stay ready, you ain't got to get ready." Sometimes you have to create it yourself, but opportunity will come, and it will come more than once. The truth of life is that it isn't always up, but it's not always down either. Life, by definition, is a series of ups and downs. It really boils down to high-quality choices. The challenge is making the right choice about which opportunity to latch onto.

A lot of people miss their "moment" because they don't invest time in preparation. Truth be told, I was scared to death when I turned down the TV audition. There was no concrete proof that it would come back around again.

Moreover, I was never able to find the right fit in Montreal. I don't speak French, and there weren't that many Black people there. To be honest, I was lonely and didn't hang out much. All I did was work. But, day by day, I learned my craft and my confidence grew.

It worked out because Montreal prepared me for that second opportunity. Looking back, I realize that because I was ready at the right time, many other doors were poised to fly open and I was able to walk in.

For a few years back then, LA was the hotbed of media-defining cultural explosions. First there was the Rodney King beating, and then a few years later, the O. J. Simpson trial captured the nation's attention. I was the most widely known Black, local news commentator at the time. When national news anchors wanted local flavor and perspective, they booked me on their shows. Those interviews caught Tom Joyner's eye, which in part led to my twice-weekly commentaries on the *Tom Joyner Morning Show.*

When BET called and asked me to audition for a new talk show, I wasn't interested. My agent told me it planned to allow 12 celebrities to guest-host the show until it could figure out who it really wanted. I was on a list that included Queen Latifah and Snoop Dogg. Don't get me wrong. I love Latifah and Snoop. But it was clear to me that if Snoop and I were on the same list as possible hosts for this new show, then BET didn't really know what it wanted the show to be.

So, I told my agent, "no way." After much cajoling from my agent, I agreed to audition, but I had one caveat—I wanted to go first. Turns out, nobody else on the list wanted to go first. So I flew to Washington, DC, confident that I could pull it off.

My first live interview threw me a bit, but it turned out to be a blessing. I have written in the past about my first guest, Russell Simmons. The question I'd asked him about rapper Tupac Shakur, who died the week prior to my start, incensed Simmons. He called me a "house nigga" live on the air and abruptly ended the interview. Everybody started tuning in just to see this guy named "Travis" who had his behind handed to him by Simmons. It took me about two years to rise above that insult but, for that first week, the controversy served me well.

The short end of the story is that after my first week, I was asked to come back again and again for 12 straight weeks. Finally my agent said to BET, "Enough. Either do the deal or not."

It did the deal.

In my five years with BET, "Tavis Smiley" became a household name with Black folk.

Trust me; your moment will come. And if you're prepared, you'll instinctively grasp the opportunity. And don't be afraid to go first.

## Three Keys to Success

This story also addresses another concern—the need to reject perceptions of our limitations. I was a public policy major with a failed political campaign on my résumé. I had no training in radio or TV.

It mattered little.

So many of us let perceptions of our limitations hold us back. Yet there are countless examples that should encourage us to dream outside our self-imposed boundaries.

By his own account, Abraham Lincoln didn't have what passed for a formal education. What he did have was a voracious appetite for books and for learning what he wasn't taught in school. Lincoln's intellectual power blazed an unpaved path to the White House.

Albert Einstein maintained that his parents were convinced that he was "retarded" because he didn't utter a word until he was three years old. Odd in youth perhaps, but the physicist, philosopher, and Nobel Laureate was not to be denied his role as a preeminent genius.

Winston Churchill was the British prime minister whose great oratory skills inspired a devastated nation during World War II. It has been written that young Churchill suffered benign parental neglect, had a speech impediment as a child, and grappled with what he defined as "the black dog" of depression. Despite his challenges, when he died in 1965, he was lionized as an honored world leader.

In his book *Outliers*, author Malcolm Gladwell unravels the secrets of extremely successful people—those "whose achievements fall outside normal experience." Chapter two dissects "The 10,000-Hour Rule." Basically, Gladwell projects that high IQs, innate talent, and training at elite institutions are not what determine one's success. Hours of practice—in fact, 10,000 hours of practice—are the amount of time researchers noted that separated the "masters" like Mozart, Bill Gates, and the Beatles from equally gifted composers, computer programmers, and musicians.

In other words, preparation—not standard education—is that extra "something" that catapults the likes of Albert Einstein, Thomas Edison, Steven Spielberg, Miles Davis, and Abraham Lincoln to fame.

Trust that inner voice, and let no thoughts of your limitations or so-called missed opportunities deter you. Focus on following the magic 10,000-hour rule. Practice and prepare without fear of failure.

In other words, get ready to be ready.

Let me close by sharing the inspiring words inscribed on the wall in the office of the late, great civil rights attorney, Johnnie Cochran:

> *"There are only three keys to success:*
> *Preparation. Preparation. Preparation."*

## TAVIS'S TAKEAWAY:

Don't be an
unprepared opportunist.
Pick your spots carefully
and prepare to win.

© Courtesy of the Tavis Smiley Collection

# CHAPTER 18

# POWER VS. PRINCIPLE

*"We have no permanent friends,*
*no permanent enemies,*
*only permanent interests."*

For years on the *Tom Joyner Morning Show*, I borrowed this phrase—adapted and adopted by the Congressional Black Caucus (CBC)—as one of my guiding philosophies. The fight for jobs, education, housing, and civil rights required strategic partnerships with legislators—friends or foes—who had to cooperate if we were to accomplish our goals.

I thought more Black folk could get where they needed to go politically and socially if they adopted this slogan.

However, after really contemplating the formulation, particularly the compromised underlying message ". . . just permanent interests" part, I became unsettled by its troubling implication.

My friend and confidante, Dr. Cornel West, was the one who originally pulled my coat and nudged me in that direction. In our conversation, he expressed flat-out disdain for the slogan. The idea that an individual or group's "interests" supersedes its "principles" troubled him greatly.

"In other words, as long as your interests are served, you'll work with anybody," Doc reasoned. "Well, what happens when your interests are antithetical to or in tension with your principles? What if your best interests betray your core truths?"

The power versus truth dynamic isn't unlike the interests versus principles dynamic. How often do we sacrifice "truth and principles" for "power and personal interests"? Doc always encourages each of us to take our own inventory. When you define and actually see your principles and values in action, it's very difficult to align yourself with individuals or situations that betray your basic beliefs.

For example, too many folks attend a particular church—knowing that the minister is a money-hungry, philandering charlatan—just because it's a popular gathering place in the community. When pressed, some hip-hop artists admit they are opposed to the violence and near-pornography they promote in their music videos. That they gain fame and fortune from their work is an impotent exchange for compromising their values.

President Obama and the Democratic Party disappointed many of their staunch supporters when they compromised on health-care reform just to appease non-appeasable

Republicans. The President still didn't pick up a single Republican vote in the Senate.

The larger point is that in each of our lives, we will be confronted with decisions that challenge our core principles. Will we choose to be "truth-tellers" or "power-grabbers"?

It's important to surround yourself with friends and associates who intellectually challenge you. There I was, accepting the precept that it's okay to swap principles for what suits our best interests until a good friend said: "Hold up, let's rethink this."

Indeed, rethinking it brought back the memory of a preeminent "truth-teller" who paid the ultimate price for solidly standing by his principles, even under tremendous fire.

## Dethroning a King

When Dr. King was murdered on the balcony of the Lorraine Motel in Memphis, Tennessee, all the evidence indicates that he departed this life believing almost everybody had turned against him.

His last two years were hell on earth. He was acceptable when he stayed within the confines of his approved role—waging the nonviolent battle for Black rights. But when he spoke out against the Vietnam War, the White House turned against him, as did leaders of the NAACP, Urban League, and other advocacy organizations. Carl Rowan and other Black writers joined their white colleagues in the denunciation of this servant-leader. His Morehouse classmates denounced him; he couldn't even get a book deal. Invitations to speak publicly declined; he was even disinvited from community speaking engagements and church-related events.

The last Harris Poll before Dr. King's death indicated that almost three-quarters of the American people had turned against him. Also at that time, more than half of all Black people opposed his stance on the Vietnam War.

Meanwhile, the Nation of Islam under Malcolm X and the Black Panther Party led by Huey P. Newton preached fiery messages of retribution that challenged the turn-the-other-cheek, nonviolent crowd. Many young Black people considered Dr. King soft, an Uncle Tom, or an antiquated relic of an increasingly irrelevant movement. The Black bourgeoisie, who feared the Baptist minister would damage their relationships with the President, were like: "Martin, what the heck are you doing?"

Let's be clear, Dr. King believed Lyndon B. Johnson was the best President of his time. The 1964 and 1965 Civil and Voting Rights Acts couldn't have been enacted without him. His admiration aside, however, Dr. King would not abandon his principles—not even to appease the most powerful man in the land and "friend of the Negro people."

This was Dr. King's standing in America when he was assassinated on April 4, 1968. The majority of whites and large numbers of bourgeois, revolutionary, and apolitical Negroes had turned against him, and he had been booted off the "most admired Americans" list.

The servant-leader, by all accounts, was persona non grata.

Now, decades later, it's generally acknowledged that the Vietnam War was the low point in the history of American military excursions. Retrospective truth, after ridicule, isolation, and personal suffering, finally validated Dr. King's principled stance.

## Principles Over Personality

It's no secret that President Bill Clinton and I are friends. When he was in office and I was on BET, he granted me more interviews than anyone else in the media—Black or white. It was clear that I had unusual access to the Clinton administration. We flew around the world together. I even traveled to Africa with him, but I was never naïve about our relationship. When he wanted to deliver a message to his Black base, his staff contacted me. There were no pretenses. He needed access to my Black audience, and I, like any other broadcaster, valued access to the White House.

Although I considered Clinton a candid straight shooter, I was also aware that the President had adopted a centrist approach for political gain. This, I've always maintained, fed his tendency to sometimes compromise too much. In spite of our mutual interests, if he disagreed with something I said, he'd let me know without getting petulant or punitive about it. We'd discuss our differences and, if necessary, would agree to respectfully disagree.

During the 1992 presidential election, then Governor Clinton sandbagged the Rev. Jesse Jackson at a Rainbow PUSH event. The candidate chose to publicly repudiate hip-hop artist and political activist Sister Souljah for controversial remarks she had made. As far as I was concerned, Clinton used Jackson's forum to let potential white voters know that he wouldn't tolerate radical Negro-ism. And that's basically what I said on the radio.

Our disagreements continued after President Clinton entered the White House. I was absolutely livid in the mid-1990s when he signed the blatantly racist 100-to-1 crack/powder cocaine crime bill with little modification. Something is fundamentally wrong with a justice system that insists on mandatory sentences for the possession of 5 grams of crack cocaine but allows folk caught with 500 grams of powdered cocaine to get off on probation.

When Clinton used poor people as pawns, signing sweeping, regressive, welfare reform proposals just to out-conservative conservatives, I took him to task. And with so many other issues—when he caved to conservative criticism and withdrew his nomination of scholar and civil rights activist Lani Guinier to be Assistant Attorney General for Civil Rights; when he dragged his feet on the Rwanda genocide crisis; and other issues affecting the poor and oppressed—I checked Bill Clinton with a vengeance.

Not to just beat up on Clinton: I also clashed with Al Gore, John Kerry, other prominent Democrats, a whole bunch of Republicans, and several Black notables. You might have noticed a familiar complaint that rises in my criticisms of presidential candidates and their parties over the years.

During a segment of CNN's *Talk Back Live* in 2000, I took presidential candidate Gore and his party to task about the way he and it kept Black voters on the low-priority shelf:

"This is real simple: The Democrats cannot win without the Black vote—period, end of sentence. Which is one of the reasons why it is so troubling . . . we have not seen the kind of time, it seems to me, (that) should be spent discussing and dissecting issues that are important, not just to the Black vote, but indeed to people of color . . . which sends a message that is less than acceptable . . . The problem is that the Democrats still too often take the Black vote for granted, and the Republicans completely ignore us."

In a forum we arranged for leading GOP presidential candidates in 2007 at Morgan State University, Arizona Sen. John McCain, former Massachusetts governor Mitt Romney, and former New York City Mayor Rudy Giuliani declined to participate. I felt their decision deserved redress:

"No one should be elected president of this country in 2008 if they think that along the way they can ignore people of color. If you want to be president of all of America, you need to speak to all Americans."

My criticisms weren't partisan; they were principled and carried a consistent message:

Don't ever let the power of anyone's personality trump your principles.

# Standing on Shallow Ground

On March 1, 1848, British statesman Henry John Temple delivered an inspiring phrase in a speech before the House of Commons:

"We have no eternal allies and we have no perpetual enemies. Our interests are eternal and perpetual, and those interests it is our duty to follow."

Somehow, when promoting the CBC's adaptation, I failed to note the altered endings.

CBC:
*"We have no permanent friends, no permanent enemies, only permanent interests."*

Temple:
*"Our interests are eternal and perpetual, and those interests it is our duty to follow."*

If I had drilled deeper, perhaps I would have realized that I was clinging to a shallow and hollow statement. It's endemic of what's wrong with our society: Everybody's dancing to the "what-have-you-done-for-me-lately" beat. But those who adopt shallow and hollow positions wind up having shallow and hollow lives. My failure was that I promulgated a philosophy that I had not wrestled with enough. It wasn't until Dr. West challenged me to dissect the words that I realized I was just using a slogan to motivate Black people to keep moving forward, making progress, and getting things done. It was a handy motto, but it was still a slogan. And slogans are not solutions. Slogans are untethered; we need to be grounded in our principles.

All too often in our society, we consider slogans and sound bites as being good enough. In fact, entire political campaigns have been built around simplistic sound bites. But in a world of one-liners, we have to make sure our phraseology actually means what we intend for it to mean. For instance, there's a whole political movement revolving around the quip "we have to take our country back."

What does that really mean?

If you really drill down, the slogan demands action— maybe even unsavory action. One has to answer *who* took their country in the first place. More important, they have to decide to what extremes—politically or personally—they will go to in order to take their country back.

In other words, sound-bite politics can lead to unsound policy or unsafe practices.

## Principles at a Price

I do not believe it's an overstatement to say that the weakened and suspect state of most media outlets is a result of its wholesale abandonment of principles. No doubt, the institution can point to a laundry list of economic and technological challenges, but it cannot boot the loss of public trust into any other camp but its own. Millions of lives might have been spared had mainstream media not buckled to post-9/11 sentiments and fully challenged former President George W. Bush's distorted reasons for invading Iraq. The Fourth Estate had an obligation to ostracize the FOX News powerhouse that altered traditional journalistic objectivity with steady streams of biased, partisan opinions and slanted news coverage.

Mainstream media mostly folded to market forces. Many large media outlets cut international coverage and in-depth investigations because they were too costly or they turned off readers, listeners, and viewers desperate for personality-driven news that validated their staid perceptions without challenge. The entire world, I maintain, has been weakened because basic media principles have been compromised.

Dr. King did not follow a "just permanent interests" philosophy. His interests were not negotiable or interchangeable. In his 1957 speech, "Give Us the Ballot," he indicted those he felt had abandoned their principles in the fight for equal voting rights:

*"The Democrats have betrayed it*
*by capitulating to the prejudices and undemocratic*
*practices of the southern Dixiecrats. The Republicans*
*have betrayed it by capitulating to the blatant hypocrisy*
*of right wing, reactionary northerners. These men*
*so often have a high blood pressure of words*
*and an anemia of deeds."*

Truth based on immutable and unshakable principles will always rise. Or as Dr. King, quoting William Cullen Bryant, said, "Truth crushed to earth will rise again."

Ultimately, we Americans are to be blamed for the way corporations, major media outlets, politicians, or political parties serve us. Without unshakable principles and standards, we become easy targets for exploitation. Popularity should never trump the will of the people. If we were truly committed to objective, uncompromised journalism, "fair and balanced" would be more than a meaningless slogan. If we really believed in a more just and equitable society, we would reject shallow and hollow mandates.

Sometimes what's in your best interest is absolutely aligned with your principles. Sometimes not. In these moments, we have to dig deep and remember the principles on which we are trying to build our lives. Make no mistake about it, if you commit to stand on your principles—like truth—the forces will try to crush you. Principles come with a price.

## TAVIS'S TAKEAWAY:

Courage is available to each of us. Your best interest must always remain in absolute alignment with your principles.

© Courtesy of the Tavis Smiley Collection

# CHAPTER 19

# WHEN EVERYBODY TURNS AGAINST YOU

**M**y tears splattered on the eight-page, single-spaced, typed letter. With each line a rip widened in my heart. The sender is celebrated around the world, yet I have the privilege to call her "friend." She's the last person from whom I expected this.

"Your spirit and your soul are out of alignment with God," she wrote.

The letter was, at least, compassionate. For months, hundreds of other notes, e-mails, calls, and news stories contained much more indicting, critical, and often life-threatening comments:

"Your ego has blinded you . . ."

"You are a sellout and a traitor to your race!"

"Smiley is a disservice to the community."

"Who died and made Tavis king? . . ."

Most of those missives poured in around February 2008. By then, candidate Barack Obama, U.S. Senator from Illinois, was emerging as the front-runner for the Democratic presidential nomination. Some of my commentaries on the *Tom Joyner Morning Show* criticized the candidate who seemed hesitant to discuss issues of specific concern to people of color. I encouraged our audience not to give the candidate a pass based on his skin color. Hold him just as accountable as we would any white candidate, I exhorted.

In late March, news spread that I was leaving Tom's show. The assumption was that pushback from Obama's angry supporters had sent me over the edge. In a statement on his show that caught me totally by surprise, Tom said I had "quit" because I couldn't "take the hate" from listeners incensed about my comments.

"People are really upset . . . he's always busting Barack Obama's chops. They call. They e-mail. They joke. They threaten. You know Tavis like I do. He needs to feel loved."

There was a lot of hate, some threats, and many insane accusations such as my punishing Obama for skipping my "State of the Black Union" forum. Another echoed the claim that I was "buck dancing" for candidate Hillary Clinton.

According to one commentator, the heat I generated in the kitchen was too much for me to bear: "For a long time, Tavis was used to people applauding him for taking tough stances . . . This was the first time he had taken a position that flat-out ticked off his core audience. But [criticism] comes with the territory."

The commentator must have missed my debut on BET. As I noted earlier, viewers definitely brought the heat after my very first interview with Russell Simmons. It took about two years to remove the boulder he placed on my shoulder when he called me a "house nigga." It took hip-hop fans a long time to stop sending angry and threatening letters, to cease showing up at public events to challenge me, and to remove the stigma attached to me, unjustly, by Simmons.

No, I can take the heat. The speculators couldn't have been more wrong.

What did sting, however, was that my years of service and my particular love for Black people seemed to have been ignored or forgotten. In reality, my position on Obama was not unlike any I had taken with presidential candidates or other politicians over the years. Frankly, this period was one of the most heated and hurtful of my entire career.

Here again, my stance wasn't personal; it was principled.

What also caused me enormous sorrow were the admonitions and warnings from colleagues, members of my staff, family, and dear friends, like the author of the eight-page letter.

Her rationale for sending it stays with me. She explained how everywhere she went—the beauty shop, the airport, or anywhere on the street—everybody was saying that I was wrong. She closed with an argument that, I suppose, indicated my misalignment with God: "Tavis, when everybody you know is pushing back, it's time to check your ego."

# Where Did It Go Wrong?

It's one thing to encourage people to find their truths, stand on principle, and adhere to the three C's (courage, conviction, and commitment) when tested. But that's a hard lesson to enact when everybody you know, love, and respect is saying you're wrong.

*"The unexamined life is not worth living."*

— S O C R A T E S

Much of my time during that most difficult period was dedicated to re-examining my reasoning, dissecting my motives, and challenging my ego. I reread every word I had ever spoken or written about Barack Obama.

Did I ever say anything to demean or disrespect him? No. Did I ever encourage voters to support his opponent? No. Did I want him to win? Yes. Do I want him to be a great President? Again, yes! I just don't like seeing Black folk ignored or taken for granted.

Perhaps, I thought, if I carefully scrutinized my record, I'd discover the radical point of departure from that which had shaped my career.

When I signed on to work with Tom Joyner in 1996, my goal was to not only make listeners think but also to find ways to move people into action mode. With a national audience of millions, we had a decent shot at creating a massive coalition of change agents.

With listener participation, we had successfully championed many causes in those first few years. Shortly after starting with Tom, I joined BET as a television host. I then had the opportunity to do double whammies—TV and radio—on certain issues and causes.

Creating, promoting, and adopting an agenda of action became my focal point. The annual "State of the Black Union" symposia, with the best and brightest minds, put us on a path to advancing a policy agenda for sustainable and positive change.

In 2006, we published the *Covenant with Black America*. It hit the #1 mark on *The New York Times* best-seller list. A year later, *The Covenant In Action*—an NAACP Image Award Winner—reached the #7 spot on the same prestigious list.

After countless radio and TV conversations, book tours, and seminars revolving around the *Covenant* books, we had thousands committed to action, armed with agenda items, corroborating statistics, bullet-point demands. We had everything we needed to barter with any established or prospective politician—Democrat or Republican—who desired our votes.

In 2007, we hosted not one, but two primetime television presidential debates on PBS—one for Democrats, at Howard University, and another for Republicans, at Morgan State University. They were the first nationally televised debates where presidential candidates exclusively addressed issues important to people of color. They were also the first that people of color—me, as moderator, and the panelists posing the questions—controlled.

By the time President Bush started his second term, we were a well-oiled machine. We knew he was on his way out and the 2008 election was going to be the mother of all elections. Our intent was to use our momentum to force candidates to address the disparities in employment, health, education, the crippling prison industrial complex, and more—everything outlined in the *Covenant with Black America.*

Who knew the candidacy of an unknown senator from Illinois would derail the wheels of our carefully crafted, collective machine?

## On the Wrong Side of History

Ironically, my mainstream audience saw no detour from my standard course. Granted, most whites don't tune into the *Tom Joyner Morning Show* or keep up with news on Black websites. Whites, for the most part, were familiar with the Tavis Smiley they knew from PBS and NPR. Some read or heard interviews with me talking about my book, *Accountable: Making America as Good as Its Promise.* Others saw or heard me say that we should treat Obama like any other presidential candidate. Many had heard about a rift between me and a large number of Black people, but they saw no justification for it in my public commentary. The majority of my white audience saw no deviation from my core beliefs expressed over the years and what they now heard me saying about Obama.

But in Black America, all of a sudden, Tavis Smiley was "stuck on stupid." Overnight I was labeled a "hater." That was the spin generated in Black media: on talk radio, the blogosphere, and other news outlets. I was the commentator who had forgotten what it means to be Black in America. I expected Obama to risk his candidacy by trumpeting himself as the "Black candidate." Later, the critics implied that I was furious because Obama wouldn't go out on the stump and promote a Black agenda.

WRONG.

I never held the position that Obama should make the woes of Black people the center of his campaign. At no time did I insist that he roll out *The Covenant*. I'm not stupid. Not only had I worked for a Black mayor who was elected five times in a city that was less than 12 percent Black, I had also run for office myself in a district that was half Black and half white. I know the danger of racial politics better than most. I also know the value of building successful political coalitions.

The perception by some of Jesse Jackson and Al Sharpton representing and caring more about the fate of Black people than the fate of all other Americans effectively doomed their respective presidential campaigns with certain voters before they even got started. No way did I expect that the presidential candidate in 2008 who happened to be Black would necessarily speak for all Black folk. Not if he expected to win the election.

I did, however, expect him—and every other candidate—to address the issues that our community raised. I said it then, and repeat it now. We cannot start a process where politicians—Black, white, or "other"—are given passes on addressing African American concerns because it might hurt their chances of getting elected. If we start that process, it can't be reversed so easily.

Judging by the increasing opposition to the nation's first Black president, it's a safe bet that, after President Obama, it will be a while before another African American occupies that office. So when a white person is back in the White House and people demand that he or she addresses their agenda, he or she can justifiably dismiss them:

"You all didn't press Obama on that particular issue, so what do you expect from me?"

There was an ugly brouhaha in early 2010 after a group of recognized African American leaders met with Obama to discuss his jobs strategy and their concerns about the unemployment crisis in Black communities. When I heard these community leaders intimate, in front of reporters and TV cameras, that the President need not articulate or even address a Black agenda, I hit the roof. I called them out publicly and organized a nationally televised symposium on C-SPAN. "We Count! The Black Agenda Is the American Agenda," took place in Chicago just weeks after their White House meeting.

These Black leaders were absolutely right when they suggested that African Americans should have their own agenda and not expect President Obama to draft it for them. Fact is, such an agenda already existed, and these leaders, as participants in the "State of the Black Union" symposia, had helped to draft it.

Furthermore, somebody has to articulate that Black agenda to the President. And frankly, if Black leaders pipe down after the President suggests he can't or won't do certain things because he wants to be reelected, then the title of "Black leader" should be summarily revoked. The same is true for leaders of other constituencies. The role and responsibility of a leader are to tell the President the truth and hold him accountable for the well-being of the people.

Before and during the firestorm, I repeated my wish that Obama succeed. But, with history as a backdrop, I reminded everyone that "great presidents aren't born, they are made." They are pushed into greatness. Without a Frederick Douglass, Abraham Lincoln wouldn't be the President history honors—neither would FDR without A. Philip Randolph or LBJ without an MLK nagging, nudging, pushing him toward his best.

If Dr. King could boldly stand for truth in spite of the fact that it meant losing favor among a substantial portion of Black people, how could I abandon my responsibility to honor his legacy and expand his universal vision?

The more I examined the timeline, it became clearer to me that I was never stuck in the stupid lane, nor was I a hater. Rather, I was simply trying to keep my promise to always speak truth to power, most especially on behalf of the people I love most.

I didn't swap my principles for my best interests. It would have been in my best interest to quietly go along just to get along. By toning it down, I might have been invited to the White House with other notable Black citizens or had President Obama as a guest on my television and radio shows regularly, the same as before he was elected President.

The more I examined the timeline, the more I realized that—cracked vessel that I am—I did not veer off my path. Prior to Obama's campaign for the White House, I had never, ever shied away from speaking my truth—no matter the odds, fallout, or blowback. As besmirched, demeaned, and denounced as I had been, I stood firm in my truth.

It's the only way I know.

## Truth Needs No Defense

Standing in my truth didn't change the fact that most of Black America considered me treasonous, and the rest were planning a funeral for my career.

When you think you're the only one who feels the way you do; when you are massively outnumbered; when everybody thinks you're wrong and those who don't say so only in whispers, never in public—doubt sets in.

When friends you've known for years write personal letters, saying: "I love you and have always supported you, but Tavis, you're wrong on this one"—doubt becomes a friend.

When your own employees start looking at you funny and questioning your good sense, and people like Tom Joyner predict that your book sales, speaking engagements, and annual income are going to drop dramatically, and it all happens— you wear doubt like a uniform.

"Tavis," my undertakers intoned, "when the history books are written, you're gonna be the odd man out."

Dr. West, who encouraged me every step of the way, offered a comforting rebuttal to the wrong-side-of-history comments: "Remember, Brother Tavis, most of the chapters on the Obama era have yet to be written. And when they are, history will have to also reflect that there were other points of view on this matter."

In the middle of all the turbulence, my mother encouraged me:

"All I can tell you is this, baby: the truth needs no defense," Mama said. "Do not feel the need, however tempted you may be, to succumb to defending yourself. The truth is the truth, and it doesn't need defending."

Another moment of comfort came during a dinner conversation with a dear friend and longtime MLK confidant who said to me, "Tavis, sometimes patience is your best friend.

There's not a whole lot you can do. You just have to tell the truth and wait it out."

As it turns out, I never did reach a point where I felt the need to make the media rounds defending myself. Staying busy, doing the work I feel I'm called to do kept me sane.

With some distance, people are starting to understand what I was talking about. They see a President handcuffed by a system designed to accommodate the rich and the lucky while the poor and unlucky live the realities of double-digit unemployment figures in their communities. They realize that the cycle of poverty that has fueled the disproportionately higher national black high-school dropout rate overstuffs the nation's prisons without redress. Many who tolerated the government's bailout of bankers and billionaires are left to wonder when Black and brown victims of the subprime mortgage tsunami will receive a little reciprocal federal love. While the President waxes poetically about improved race relations, rising racial tensions betray the "post-racial" illusion. Suddenly, people of color realize that the concerns of a paranoid populace are of top priority while their sentiments seem like an afterthought in the milieu of "hope and change." The late Michael Jackson's "Earth Song," with the haunting "what about us?" refrain, has become a reverberating theme among African Americans. They wonder why their issues don't seem to resonate with the Obama administration. So far, they've seen a Black President preside over the dismantling of the discriminatory

"Don't Ask, Don't Tell" antigay military mandate. They've heard Obama and Secretary of State Hillary Clinton reassure Israel that it has the United States' support, even as it builds settlements that have been widely condemned for stoking dangerous embers in the region.

Yet issues that Black leaders and the Congressional Black Caucus have championed for years, such as reform of the criminal justice system go unaddressed. We cannot afford to ignore a criminal justice system that disproportionately targets and incarcerates Black and brown people.

The CBC has long taken federal contracting programs that bypass Black businesses and favor white enterprises to task. According to the Ohio State University–based Kirwin Institute, white-owned businesses received 82.1 percent of stimulus contracts compared to 3.4 percent for Black-owned businesses. Is it really too much to ask that this important issue be addressed instead of being given short shrift or totally dismissed?

The Obama administration's answer to the economic crisis that Black people face dates back almost 50 years. President John F. Kennedy is credited with the aphorism "a rising tide lifts all boats." The slogan also served as President Ronald Reagan's justification for his "trickle-down" policies—the assumption that relief for upper-income Americans, specifically tax relief, will trickle down and lift up the poor. In a word, it's baloney. Better yet, it's what George H. W. Bush described as "voodoo economics" while campaigning against Reagan for the presidency.

In December 2009, after Obama had pushed through his stimulus package, he was specifically asked how it was going to help Black people, and he gave the "lift all boats" response: ". . . I can't pass laws that say I'm just helping Black folks. I'm the President of the United States. What I can do is make sure that I am passing laws that help all people, particularly those who are most vulnerable and most in need. That in turn is going to help lift up the African-American community."

Really? How exactly did that statement reconcile with a national unemployment rate at the time of 8.8 percent for whites and a jobless rate of 15.6 percent for adult African Americans, and nearly 43.5 percent among Black youth? In 2009, only 4 out of 100 low-income Black students were able to find work. How exactly did the stimulus help the most vulnerable and those in need?

"A rising tide does not necessarily lift all boats," wrote economist Abdullah Shibli, "for example, boats that have a hole or need to be otherwise repaired." The closing paragraph of Shibli's February 2010 commentary in *The Daily Star* was written as a personal plea to Obama:

"So, Mr. President, a rising tide does not lift all boats. Some boats suffer damages, some lose their occupants, and others become too costly to run. And while the big boats and newer boats can sail away, the ones that stay behind need a little help to join the rest to sail out."

My own view is that all the boats did not go down at the same time, and all the boats will not come up at the same time. Wall Street and Harlem are both on the same island called Manhattan. The former has definitely come up, the later is still drowning. And finally, when the tide does come up if you're in a yacht and I'm in a dinghy, we still have a serious problem.

To summarize, my initial concerns about those small boats perpetually grounded in low tide have become the shared fears of a growing number of people. Namely, if we're not forever vigilant, there is an imminent possibility that symbolism will trump substance in the Obama era.

With the 2012 presidential election zooming toward us, many Black people are reflecting on the 2008 campaign. Prior to that historic election, millions who listened to the *Tom Joyner Morning Show* supported and pushed a Black agenda called the *Covenant with Black America*. At that time, they demanded that *all* presidential candidates address Black folks' issues outlined in *The Covenant*.

The call for accountability and the need for a Black agenda are as relevant now as ever.

Truth is not seasonal.

So, what do you do when everybody turns against you?

Have patience, stay strong, and stand in your truth.

# Dear Friend . . .

I sat down with a broken heart and moistened eyes to respond to my dear friend's letter. Dr. King's trials and tribulations and that lonely, ostracized place he occupied before his death played in my head like an old reel-to-reel movie.

Please don't think I'm placing myself on the mantel with Dr. King. Hardly. It's just that Dr. King, Gandhi, many others, and even Jesus Christ are testaments to the fact that when you challenge power, when you stand up for the disenfranchised, the dispossessed, and discarded, you may stand alone.

My response was short, about two paragraphs. I thanked her for her letter, which I wanted to believe was written out of genuine concern for me. At the risk of remaining unaligned with God, I wrote: "I will hold fast to my beliefs."

In truth, I was never really alone. Throughout the Obama drama, there were always a few who held me up when my knees almost buckled. One of them called in the midst of my storm. She too is world renowned, only her forte is music. I wasn't home when she called and left me these encouraging words on my voicemail from one of my favorite hymns.

It was the first stanza of a song written by Thomas Shepherd:

*"Must Jesus bear the cross alone,*
*And all the world go free?*
*No, there's a cross for everyone,*
*And there's a cross for me."*

## TAVIS'S TAKEAWAY:

Love wins.

© Vandell Cobb

# CHAPTER 20

# FATHER
# KNOWS BEST

I interviewed Barack Obama many times in the years prior to his becoming President. I was never quite sure how he felt about it, but I always found myself at some point in our conversations bringing up his first unsuccessful race for the U.S. Congress. There's a reason.

Here's a quick refresher: In 1999, Barack Obama— a lawyer, former community organizer-turned Illinois State Senator—set his sights on Congress. The seat's occupant was, and still is, Bobby Rush, former Black Panther and perennially elected incumbent from Chicago's South Side.

Obama was trounced by a two-to-one margin.

A few years after he was handily defeated by Rush, Obama entered the U.S. Senate race and won, becoming the only African American among the 100 senators. With the audacity of hope, he set out on a quest to be elected the nation's first African American president.

He runs.

He wins.

He makes history.

Who knew?

Apparently, God knew.

You see, Obama's story fascinated me because my story, your story, and a whole lot of other people's stories serve as examples of one of the most common human failures. It's one that I repeated often throughout my life until I finally got it: The hardheaded failures that accompanied my increasingly complex plans for myself always wound up being far less than what God had in mind for me.

Over the years, I have had to finally learn how to let go, to realize that I don't dictate the journey—I never have. Like the time I was ready to abandon California because the job I expected wasn't there when I arrived. Because things didn't go as I had planned, I thought something was wrong with me. Ever had that feeling? Because things aren't working out just right that there must be something wrong with you, right?

There was nothing wrong with me. And there's probably nothing wrong with you.

It was part of His plan. I am now celebrating 20 years in broadcasting. There have been many incredible achievements that I've been blessed to accomplish along the way. The plans

I've made for my life are good, but never as good as what God had planned for me.

It's impossible for me to share a book about the lessons I've learned without coming full circle. There are three things, I maintain, that sustain us. I refer to them as "the three F's"—Faith, Family, and Friends. My family and friends are crucial and very important to me. But faith trumps all.

My unyielding faith has been fortified by a Father who accepted my occasionally troubling turns, my huge misses of the mark, yet who never stopped responding to my human folly with exactly what He knew was best for me. No matter how much I tried to tell God what to do.

## You Almighty

The concept of the movie, *Bruce Almighty*, is absolutely brilliant. Jim Carrey plays Bruce, a faithless guy who learns the meaning of faith by becoming God. The movie's "God," played by Morgan Freeman, lends Bruce His powers to teach him a lesson.

As the Almighty, Bruce has to learn the downside of using his powers for personal gratification. But true to His nature, God gave Bruce all the powers of the universe, except one—the ability to tamper with an individual's free will.

Consequently, Bruce, even with his infinite authority, could not make the woman in his life love him for life.

She alone has the power to choose love. Or not.

That's heavy. The underlying message: You can't fade free will. We have all been granted the divine privilege to choose our destinies.

But our gifts don't end with free will. We also have the benefit of claiming our blessings. It's not about how educated, connected, popular, wealthy, or attractive you may be—God grants grace and mercy to all. You can't buy it, steal it, or sell it. You can, however, put yourself in the position to receive it, but you can't earn it. *He* chooses who will be extended grace and mercy. It is an unmerited favor.

I wrote earlier about the advice Mayor Tom Bradley gave me—"all things being equal," the person who looks the best will win out. Although I understand the societal implication of his advice, thankfully there is no "all things being equal" clause when it comes to God's grace and mercy. The fact is, even when things *aren't* equal, if it's meant for you to receive God's grace, you're going to get it. The world can't give it, and the world can't take it away. I know because I've been the recipient of countless blessings that I didn't deserve or earn.

Talk about meritocracy; grace is the ultimate example. It is gifted to all.

Now, as the Parable of the Talents demonstrates, you can give your talent away or let it go to waste, but no one can take from you what God has for you.

Success in some ways is what each of us determines it to be. To me, success is the rock-solid knowledge that your gifts are in motion, that you are an engaged, activated, and organic part of God's universal plan.

## Concentrate on You

In the movie, Bruce, as God, has to sift through millions of prayers and is burdened with the responsibility of deciding who receives blessings and who's left out.

In real life, a lot of us feel left out or denied. It doesn't seem fair. Especially when we see certain folk who appear to be advancing beyond us economically, socially, or culturally who we believe can't possibly be walking in the favor of God.

Well, I can tell you two things. One, I feel you. I too have looked at God a little funny at times and said, "You can't be serious! Him? Her? Oh, c'mon, Lord!" And yet, two, I know and accept that "God reigns over the just as well as the unjust." In other words, some folk act a fool and God still bestows grace upon them, too. Remember, grace is an unmerited favor.

So, what to do? Here's where we cue Jeffrey Osborne and a group called LTD: "Concentrate on You." When you're busy concentrating on you and making your own creations in the world, you have less time to be distracted by what other folks are doing or saying.

Each morning I revitalize and reenergize my soul with this sustaining prayer, courtesy of my dear friend, Dr. Gardner C. Taylor:

*"Lord, when the evening comes and the night falls,*
*let me be able to look back on this day and find*
*something I have done which I can present to you,*
*that might not make me feel so ashamed."*

Every time I pray this prayer, I get reminded of who I am and whom I'm trying to please. When it looks like other folks are advancing ahead of me; when it looks like others are blessed instead of me; when nothing seems to be going right and the world seems cruel and upside down—I concentrate on me. And I recommit myself to doing the best I can, with what I have, right where I am. This, I believe, is all that is required of us.

## Something Bigger

The decay of our civilization and the devolution of our culture are constant concerns for me. Yet in the midst of all the madness, there are signs, small signals that we are perhaps evolving in the right direction. Some people do understand that power is not the path to peace, and money is an artificial substitute for happiness. Some people do understand the difference between success and greatness. Said Dr. King, "Everybody can be great because anybody can serve . . . You only need a heart full of grace. A soul generated by love."

It's not always easy, but I choose to look for the light in this world full of darkness. Most often, against myriad obstacles, this light is being shined by everyday people. But sometimes, even by the rich and the lucky, too.

The "Giving Pledge"—the brainchild of Bill Gates and Warren Buffett that so far has received commitments from 40 billionaires to donate half their fortunes to charity—is an encouraging sign. The movement has so many potential benefits. It may persuade other wealthy individuals to utilize their wealth in holistic ways to promote the power of philanthropy.

I adhere to the Biblical edict that "to whom much is given, much is required." I have been blessed beyond measure in my life. Trying to give back is reciprocity for my many blessings. It's the rent I pay for the space that I occupy. I'm convinced abundant blessings will continue as long as I strive to bless others.

I pride myself on my discipline and being in tune with myself. I'm not a vacillator, nor do I waffle; I know what I believe in and what I want. But there have been times when I really didn't know which way was up or which way to go. That's why having my relationship with God is so vitally important.

I just don't know how people navigate through life without having somebody or something that they can believe in or call upon in those moments when they're stuck. When friends and family have abandoned them. When everybody has turned against them. When plans go so terribly awry. When there's no place to turn. When we fail and fall flat on our faces; what gets us through?

There was no clearer answer than the story of 33 Chilean miners trapped some 2,000 feet underground for nearly ten weeks. For 17 days, no one knew if they were dead or alive. Once found, the world watched with bated breath as intricate plans were made to lift the men from dangerously fragile surroundings. Finally, on Wednesday, October 13, 2010, the miracle survivors were lifted from the San Jose mine. One by one, each testified to the powerful force that cradled them throughout the ordeal:

"I held on to God's hand. At no point in time did I doubt that God would get me out of there," said Mario Sepulveda, 40, the second miner lifted to safety.

Jimmy Sanchez, 19, felt a need to correct those who insisted 33 souls were trapped beneath the earth: "There are actually 34 of us because God has never left us down here," Sanchez said.

Miner José Ojeda had a hard time explaining his feelings. There was no doubt in his mind that God had sustained them for a reason; he just wasn't sure what that reason is . . . yet.

"Here we have different faiths, all brothers in God . . . If God allows us to live, it is because of something he has prepared for us when we come out."

I love Ojeda's acceptance of the unknown. There's no need to sweat the *whys* or the *wherefores*. He understands. It's the score of a song I adore, "I Understand," performed by Smokie Norful. He does understand. We can trust His plan even when we can't hear His voice.

Now that's blessed assurance!

All I know is that I could not have survived 20 years in this chaotic, fleeting, ever-changing world of mass communications without something bigger than me to sustain and guide me.

I have not arrived at this blessed place with a contented sense of contribution and peace of mind because I'm the smartest, the most talented, the most connected, or the luckiest.

Big Mama used to say all the time in her broken English, "It ain't no good luck; it's a good God!"

Thank goodness, there is something in the universe bigger and greater than Tavis. Because I know this, I'm okay with the fact that I'm not human and divine—just human. As such, I know I'm going to fail from time to time. Here then is the question I've learned to wrestle with daily: How good is my failure? I'm okay with this formulation because I know that my Father always knows best and wants only the best for me. And that's really all I need to know to keep it moving. To keep working every day to get better.

And that's why the words of Samuel Beckett resonate so with me: "Ever tried. Ever failed. No matter. Try again. Fail again. Fail better."

## TAVIS'S TAKEAWAY:

Even when you can't
hear His voice,
you can trust His plan.

# GRATITUDE

**W**ith deep gratitude, I first thank Denise Pines for encouraging me to share the stories in this book.

A very special thanks to Sylvester Brown, Jr. for his insights and hard work in the completion of this project.

Much appreciation to Cheryl Woodruff and the team at SmileyBooks for shepherding this project through to completion on time.

To Louise Hay, Reid Tracy, and all the good people at Hay House, thank you for being such a great partner.

Finally, to my staff at The Smiley Group, Inc., thanks for everything each of you did to help me deliver a book of which we can all be proud—most especially, Danny Miles Davis, Dawn Fong, Kimberly Logan, Kimberly McFarland, Rhonda Nelson, Patrick Thomas, and Darryl Wesson.

# ABOUT THE
# AUTHOR

From his celebrated conversations with world figures, to his work to inspire the next generation of leaders, as a broadcaster, author, advocate, and philanthropist, **Tavis Smiley** continues to be an outstanding voice for change. Currently, Smiley hosts the late night television talk show, *Tavis Smiley* on PBS, *The Tavis Smiley Show* distributed by Public Radio International (PRI), and is the co-host of *Smiley & West* (PRI). He is the first American to simultaneously host signature talk shows on both public television and public radio. In addition to his radio and television work, Smiley has authored fourteen books, including the book he edited, *Covenant with Black America*, which became the first nonfiction book by a Black-owned publisher to reach #1 on *The New York Times* bestseller list. He is also the presenter and creative force behind America I AM: *The African American Imprint*—an unprecedented traveling museum exhibition celebrating the extraordinary impact of African American contributions to our nation and to the world. In 2009, *TIME* magazine named him to their list of "The World's 100 Most Influential People." This year, 2011, marks his 20th year in broadcasting.

# NOTES

# NOTES

## SMILEYBOOKS TITLES OF RELATED INTEREST

### BOOKS

*THE COVENANT In Action*
Compiled by Tavis Smiley

*AMERICA I AM LEGENDS:*
*Rare Moments and Inspiring Words*
Edited by SmileyBooks • Introduction by Tavis Smiley

*NEVER MIND SUCCESS . . . GO FOR GREATNESS!*
*The Best Advice I've Ever Received*
by Tavis Smiley

*HOPE ON A TIGHTROPE*
*Words & Wisdom*
by Cornel West

*PEACE FROM BROKEN PIECES:*
*How to Get Through What You're Going Through*
by Iyanla Vanzant

*BLACK BUSINESS SECRETS:*
*500 Tips, Strategies and Resources for African American Entrepreneurs*
by Dante Lee

*BRAINWASHED:*
*Challenging the Myth of Black Inferiority*
by Tom Burrell

### DVDs/CDs

*STAND:* a film by Tavis Smiley

*ON AIR*
*The Best of Tavis Smiley on the Tom Joyner Morning Show 2004–2008*
4-CD commemorative set with booklet

All of the above are available at your local bookstore,
or may be ordered online through Hay House
(see contact information on next page)

We hoped you enjoyed this SMILEYBOOKS publication.
If you would like to receive additional information, please contact:

## SB

SMILEYBOOKS

Distributed by:
Hay House, Inc.
P.O. Box 5100
Carlsbad, CA 92018-5100
**(760) 431-7695** or **(800) 654-5126**
**(760) 431-6948 (fax)** or **(800) 650-5115 (fax)**
**www.hayhouse.com®** • **www.hayfoundation.org**

*Published and distributed in Australia by:* Hay House Australia Pty. Ltd. •
18/36 Ralph St. • Alexandria NSW 2015 • Phone: 612-9669-4299 •
Fax: 612-9669-4144 • www.hayhouse.com.au

**Published and distributed in the United Kingdom by:** Hay House UK, Ltd. •
292B Kensal Rd., London W10 5BE • Phone: 44-20-8962-1230 •
Fax: 44-20-8962-1239 • www.hayhouse.co.uk

**Published and distributed in the Republic of South Africa by:** Hay House SA (Pty), Ltd.,
P.O. Box 990, Witkoppen 2068 • Phone/Fax: 27-11-467-8904 •
info@hayhouse.co.za • www.hayhouse.co.za

**Published and Distributed in India by:** Hay House Publishers India,
Muskaan Complex, Plot No. 3, B-2, Vasant Kunj, New Delhi 110 070 •
Phone: 91-11-4176-1620 • Fax: 91-11-4176-1630 • www.hayhouse.co.in

**Distributed in Canada by:** Raincoast • 9050 Shaughnessy St., Vancouver, B.C.
V6P 6E5 • Phone: (604) 323-7100 • Fax: (604) 323-2600